How to have **Real Faith**

In the True God

How <u>not</u> to be
'Children of a Lesser God'

By David Mathis

Cover Photo: Hubble hs-2004-41-a-full_tif A photo of a supernova near a star which is pulling matter from the supernova. What an amazing God we have!

All scripture quotations are from the King James Version with antiquated words updated by the author.

Table of Contents

Acknowledgments

Without my Dad, Calvin Franklin (Frank) Mathis, this book couldn't have been written. He is the genius behind the allegories and most of the theology. He has written many papers proving his points in his goal to help people get a better picture of the true God of the Bible. Although he had always attended a Christian Church, he really became a believer while he was attending Moody Bible Institute and became a pilot-mechanic. He married Phyllis Dorene Smith and joined Wycliffe Bible Translators' Jungle Aviation and Radio Service. He was sent to Peru where Mom joined him after Becky, my older sister, was born. I was born in Peru a year and nine months later. Wycliffe started opening up Ecuador and we moved there where my brother Timothy was born. Dad worked with Nate Saint and flew one of the sorties looking for the Aucas.

We came home on furlough in September of 1955 and found that my maternal grandmother had no one to take care of her. She hadn't been able to walk since her thirties because of rheumatoid arthritis. Dad decided that it was his responsibility to take care of her after reading what Paul said in 1 Timothy 5:8 *But if any provide not for his own, and especially for those of his own house, he has denied the faith, and is worse than an infidel.*

In January of 1956 Nate Saint, Jim Elliot, Ed McCully, Peter Fleming, and Roger Youderian were killed by the Aucas, now known as the Waorani. I remember the day Mom and Dad received the news even though I was only four years old at the time. I wasn't sure what had happened but I remember them both crying.

Dad worked at Douglas and Autonetics and had Bible studies at lunch time at work, and in the evenings in different people's homes. We attended a number of churches but most did not like his views on the sovereignty of God. We finally started attending Grace Brethren in Long Beach, California where Dr. David Hocking was the pastor. Dad really appreciated him and would send him letters from time to time with a different take on a passage on which Dr. Hocking had preached. He would always reply and many times agreed with Dad.

Dad started his own business in 1977 making automatic gate operators and hiring many ex-cons. He taught twenty-nine years in a prison ministry at Terminal Island Prison. As prisoners were transferred to other prisons, they wrote to Dad and he started a correspondence course for prisoners which he still continues. After they finish eight lessons Dad sends them a free study Bible. He has sent out over thirty-eight hundred Bibles in the last five years to over eighty prisons.

At eighty years of age he stopped visiting Terminal Island because of the commute and the fact that the chaplain often wouldn't show up to let him in. At eighty-seven he continues to care for Mom who has been an invalid since 2003, make parts for the company he sold in

2006, and answer up to one hundred letters per week from prisoners.

I will always be grateful for the way I was raised. Dad was a strict disciplinarian but had unconditional love for all of us. It has been easy to have a proper view of God because of his example.

I also want to thank my wonderful mom who led me to Jesus at age five and spent countless hours talking with me about every subject under the sun, but always came back to Jesus. For many years she had three Bible clubs a week: elementary, junior high, and high school. She was an amazing woman with plenty of love to go around. She has been unable to speak for many years and I miss our conversations.

I also wish to thank those who helped to edit this book: Jim Brumbach, Charmaine Coatney, Mark Goens, Frank Mathis, Barbara Roberts, and Jim Stublefield. This does not mean that all of them agree completely with this book, but I appreciate very much their time, talents, and comments.

Dedication

I am dedicating this book to my sweet wife Janet, without whom life would be much less enjoyable and with whom I am more in love than ever; to my son Jesse, his wife Shannon, their children Caleb and Piper; my older daughter Sarah, her husband Josh, their four daughters, Katie, Hailey, Breanna , and Becky; my youngest daughter Joylyn , her husband Keith (Ollie), and their three boys Carver, Zane, and Sylas; with the prayer that each of them will love and serve the true God with their whole heart so they can truly love and serve others.

Foreword

As I begin this short book on faith, I am sitting in a recliner recovering from three broken ribs, with five stitches in the back of my head, and a dislocated wrist with three pins in it. I think this is God's way of slowing me down to finally write something I have long felt was important. I take full responsibility for my fall but realize that it was God's plan as well. God claims in His Word to be in full control of all things and I simply believe Him.

I am not a great theologian; I am a simple jack-of-all-trades Bible teacher, who has been a pastor for the last eight years. God has given me the gift of teaching, and a simple mind which helps me to "put the cookies on the lower shelf where the kids can reach them," as Dr. McGee used to say. I don't ask you to believe what I write about God just because I say so, but to believe what God wrote about Himself in His Word. I expect you to *"search the scriptures to see if these things are so."* The aim of this writing is for you to find complete confidence in God's salvation, true victory over sin in your walk with Jesus, absolute peace, unlimited trust in God, in and through your circumstances, and total confidence in the Holy Spirit as you witness to others.

Many believers and non-believers alike think that faith is the power of positive thinking; meaning that we make something become true simply by believing it. This is what Hollywood has been pushing ever since "Yes, Virginia, there is a Santa Claus". There is some benefit in the power of positive thinking, as optimists will usually get more accomplished than pessimists, but that has nothing to do with real faith.

Some people say faith is a "leap in the dark", but that is pure stupidity. No one in their right mind would take a leap without evidence that shows there is a good place to land. While it is true that we cannot put God in a test tube, we can prove to anyone with an open mind that God exists and the Bible is accurate. Most atheists do not want to believe in a god because then they would be responsible to him. They certainly don't want to believe in the God of the Bible, who has laws and who sends sinners to hell.

A friend of mine named Jim Brumbach had a philosophy professor years ago who showed all the faults in each religion as he taught. He finished with Christianity and said, "There are no internal or external flaws in Christianity."

He proceeded to prove the truth of the Bible until one student cried out, "Don't push your Christianity on us."

"I'm not a Christian," he replied.

The student was very surprised and asked. "Why not, if you think it's true?"

"I don't want to live that way," replied the professor.

At least he was honest in his refusal to trust; most are not and don't really check out the claims of Christ.

If I wanted to go my own way and not believe that I am responsible to God, I would have to believe that He does not exist. If I really wanted to believe that God does not exist, I would need to convince others to agree with me. From this idea came our modern atheistic and evolutionary schooling.

What is faith?
Many believers say, "God said it, I believe it; that settles it." While that is true for salvation and victory, "God said it, that settles it" is really enough for most things. Everything God says is true whether or not I believe it. Generally it does me no good unless I believe it, but whether or not I believe it does not change its veracity.

Personally, I like the FAITH acronym: **F**orsaking **A**ll **I** **T**rust **H**im. I no longer trust anything else to get to Heaven. My trust is in Jesus alone for salvation, peace, purpose, fulfillment, joy, eternal life, sanctification (a big word meaning I am set apart from the world and its ways, and set apart for God's purposes), and a host of other things.

Remember that faith is not just mental assent. I cannot believe in Jesus like I believe in George Washington and be saved. Faith in a chair causes me to sit in the chair. Faith in the engineers and mechanics causes me to get on an airplane. Proper faith causes me to put all my weight on the object of my faith.

Introduction

I remember hearing a story of a very large and expensive printing press which was bought by a company in South America from a company in the United States many years ago. After about a month it started having a problem and finding themselves unable to clear up the problem by telegraph, the company dispatched their best engineer immediately. When he arrived he was not allowed to touch the machine because the owner thought him much too young. The owner directly cabled the company in the U. S. asking for someone older and received the following reply: "Let him repair it, he designed it."

We have been "fearfully and wonderfully made" by God Almighty. He designed us to know and glorify Him. We should give Him complete control of our lives because He designed and created us and knows us intimately. He told us about Himself in His Word and sent Jesus to die for us and rise again giving us salvation, forgiveness, power over sin, unspeakable joy, and eternal life. Yet so often we don't follow our Designer and Creator, and worse, we try to remake Him the way we want to see Him instead of the awesome and dreadful God He is. Of course He is compassionate, loving, and merciful, but we tend to accentuate the attributes we like and discount the attributes we do not.

I hope in this short book to bring us back to the place where we may have a more balanced view of our King of kings and Lord of lords so that we come to the place where we trust Him completely. If we fear God properly we have nothing else to fear. 1 John 4:18 *There is no fear in love; but perfect love casts out fear: because fear has torment. He that fears is not made perfect in love.* Life without fear, life without worry, but life full of excitement serving the King and having a close relationship with Him as His child, is the life we are offered. So often we settle for a lesser god, who cannot be completely trusted, who "allows" bad things to come into our lives that he really doesn't want to happen, who is subject to our whims and desires and the sins of those who hurt us. He is not the God of the Bible, though he appears to be the god of most Americans.

So the reason for this book is to start to show what it takes to have real faith in the God that He claims to be in His Word. This short book is far from complete, but I think that it is a start in the right direction. May God bless you with a greater understanding of Who He really is, as you read, and may your awe of Him, love for Him, and trust in Him, grow.

Chapter One

Faith That Saves

What does it take for a person to be saved and have the confidence that they already have eternal life and when they die they will be with Jesus? What kind of faith really saves you?

I remember in high school our youth group going on a "Beach Reach'" in Long Beach, California armed with some *Four Spiritual Laws* pamphlets. I am quite sure that the boy with whom I spoke did not become a believer at that point. He read through the booklet and said the prayer with me, but I do not think that he really put his faith in Jesus as his Savior.

Don't misunderstand; God could have saved him then or used some of what I had said that day, later in his life; God can do whatever He wants. I am just saying that getting him to say a prayer did not save him.

The Bible does not say to say a prayer or to ask Jesus into your heart. Many Christians use Revelation 3:20 *"Behold I stand at the door and knock, if anyone hears My voice and opens the door, I will come in to him and eat with him and he with Me,"* to say that we need to invite Jesus into our hearts. We always need to check the context of the verse. This verse has nothing to do with salvation and is written not to unbelievers, but to believers who are not having fellowship with Jesus. Jesus wants us to invite Him in to every part of our lives so that our whole being has fellowship with Him.

To receive salvation we first need to repent. To some, that is a scary word. It simply means to re-think or to change one's mind or to turn around. I remember when I was working at a gas station in Sunny Valley, Oregon, just north of Grants Pass where I currently live, that a family came in to fill up and asked a strange question, "How far is it to Idaho?"

"I'm not sure," I replied, "That is the first time anyone has asked."

"But it can't be far," they protested, "We left Eugene two hours ago!"

It was my sad duty to tell them that they had chosen the wrong freeway, heading south instead of east, and were now farther from their destination than when they started. They were very sincere about what they were doing, but sincerity does no good unless you are on the right road going in the right direction. They could never arrive in Idaho unless they repented and turned around to drive the right direction.

> Sincerity does no good unless you are on the right road going in the right direction.

Some modern day preachers wouldn't have wanted to disappoint them, and would have told them just to keep going because all roads lead to Idaho. Without repentance there can be no salvation because there is nothing from which to be saved. If I don't turn to go toward Jesus, I have not been saved.

From what should we be repenting? Each of us is born selfish. We think of that as normal because it is natural and we all deal with it. My wife and I have nine grandchildren and it is so easy to see the selfishness in each of them. Our oldest granddaughter, Katie, is eight. When her sister Hailey was still a baby and she was about three years old, they were up visiting. Katie wasn't being very careful with her sister so I started reminding her, "Katie, think about Hailey."

This went on throughout the day and that night when I said it again she turned exasperated to me and said, "But when do I get to think about Katie?"

That is exactly where we are naturally–thinking about ourselves and putting ourselves first and–God calls that sin. In point of fact every sin we commit comes from our selfishness and pride. This is why we need to repent, to turn from our sin and turn to Jesus.

This is not "Lordship Salvation", which says that if Jesus is not lord of all, He is not lord at all; basically saying that if you are not living right you are not going to Heaven. That is a works salvation which takes us back to before the Reformation. What I am talking about is true Godly repentance, Godly sorrow for sin and a desire to change direction. This is not based on performance, but on faith being transferred from self to God for salvation.

In Acts 3:19 Peter tells the people in his audience how to be saved: *"Repent therefore, and be converted, that your sins may be blotted out."* Sadly, repentance is left out of most preaching today, but God still hates sin, Jesus still died for sin, and without repentance there is no salvation. The reason so many refuse salvation is that we have to admit we are wrong, that we can't fix it, and ask God to fix us. Any other religion or cult will allow you some dignity; you can do something to please their god; but the God of the Bible says in Psalm 14:3 *They are all gone aside, they are all together become filthy: there is none that does good, no, not one.* We are morally and spiritually bankrupt, and we need to come on that basis. But repentance alone will not save you.

One of the clearest passages on salvation occurs in the book of Acts when the Philippian jailer asked Paul what he had to do to be saved. Paul replied in Acts 16:31, *"Believe on the Lord Jesus Christ and you will be saved."* It is not a prayer that saves you, it is not asking Jesus into your heart; it is not being good or going to church; the only thing that saves you is believing in Jesus. That means believing everything He said about Himself, His Father, the Holy Spirit, and about us.

Jesus made it very clear that He is the only way when He said in John, *"I am the way, the truth, and the life; no one comes to the Father but by Me."* Our faith must be in Him and in Him alone to have eternal life. Of course, it is a good idea to pray and confess your sin and thank God for His forgiveness, but it is your faith, not the prayer that saves you.

Now let's go a step back because we have been talking about salvation from man's perspective. Let's take a look from God's perspective. God says that no one really seeks Him. Romans 3:10 *As it is written, There is none righteous, no, not one: there is none that understands, there is none that seeks after God.*

We know that a lot of people claim to seek God, but all of them fall into one of two categories. The larger category is made up of those who are seeking for a god that will satisfy them. They are looking for a god made in their image, a god like Aaron made when Moses was up on Mount Sinai and the people asked him to make one for them. What kind of god did he make? He made a calf of gold. Why? Because an ox is a servant and a calf is even easier to control. That is what these seekers want: a god that pleases them, not the Almighty God of the Bible whose name is "Warrior" and "Jealous", who demands strict allegiance, and says, *"Be holy; for I am holy."* 1 Peter 1:16.

The smaller category is made up of those whose names were written in the Lamb's Book of Life before the foundation of the world, but have not yet believed. There are others who were not written in the book before the foundation of the world: Revelation 17:8 *Whose names were not written in the book of life from the foundation of the world.* But the seekers we are talking about are those whose names were written in the book and the Father is drawing them, but they have not yet believed. Ephesians 1:4 *According as He hath chosen us in Him before the foundation of the world, that we should be holy and without blame before Him.*

Jesus said in John 6:44, *"No man can come to me, except the Father Who has sent Me draw him: and I will raise him up at the last day."* Jesus is clearly saying that it is not in man to come to God, and indeed man is incapable of coming to Jesus unless drawn by the Father. Literally, "drawn" would be translated "dragged" and it is the same word used of forcing a person to court as in James 2:6 *Do not rich men oppress you, and <u>draw</u> you before the judgment seats?*

 Some say that John 12:31, 32 says that everyone is drawn. *Now is the judgment of this world: now shall the prince of this world be cast out. And I, if I be lifted up from the earth, will draw all men unto Me.* But notice that here it is Jesus drawing, not the Father, and the context is judgment not salvation. Jesus is the judge as the Father has made Him so; Jesus will draw all men to judgment. John 5:22 *For the Father judges no man, but has committed all judgment unto the Son.* However, only those whom the Father draws can come to Jesus and they will come.

 And in John 6:65 Jesus clarifies further: *And He said, "Therefore said I unto you, that no man <u>can</u> come unto Me, except it were given unto him of My Father."* "Given" could be translated "bestowed" or "granted." So we do not have the ability to come to Jesus unless the Father draws us and grants us permission and then we will come. . In John 6:37 Jesus said, *"<u>All</u> that the Father gives Me <u>shall come to Me</u>; and he that comes to Me I* *will in no way cast out."* These seekers are only seeking because the Father is drawing them and will, at some point, give them efficacious grace, which means effective grace, or grace that accomplishes and from which the receiver will not turn Matthew 22:14 *"For many are called, but few are chosen."*

In other words, those whom the Father draws and gives this special grace will come to Christ and no others can. This takes the decision out of our hands and leaves it with God. This is why we cannot lose our salvation. If it was based on our decision we could change our minds. Those who believe in both free will and eternal security are not being logical or biblical.

That last phrase in John 6:37 *"He that comes to Me I will in no way cast out"* is used by many to say that there must be free will. Another verse is Revelation 22:17 *"And the Spirit and the bride say, 'Come'. And let him that hears say, 'Come'. And let him that is athirst come. And whosoever will, let him take the water of life freely."* This verse is also used to say that there must be free will. Neither verse says that we can come of our own free will. As we

> "Whosoever will may come," but we are all born "whosoever won'ts".

have seen in the scriptures, we are all born "whosoever won'ts". We refuse to come to God because we have a sin nature. The pride in us says, "I would rather do it myself." We will not come to God unless He changes us.

Saying that these passages even suggest free will is like saying that God gave us the law expecting us to keep it. Galatians 3:24 *Wherefore the law was our schoolmaster to bring us unto Christ, that we might be justified by faith.* It is abundantly clear from this passage that the law was given to show us our depravity and our need for Christ. The passages throwing open the door to salvation do the same. Salvation is freely available to all who would come, but none of us want to come until we are regenerated.

Martin Luther, one of the greatest reformers, said, "If any man ascribes anything of salvation, even the very least, to the free will of man, he knows nothing of grace, and he has not learned Jesus Christ correctly."

C.H. Spurgeon, one of the greatest preachers in recent history, said, "I do not come into this Pulpit hoping that perhaps somebody will of his own free will return to Christ. My hope lies in another quarter. I hope that my Master will lay hold of some of them and say, 'You are Mine, and you shall be Mine. I claim you for Myself.' My hope arises from the freeness of Grace, and not from the freedom of the will."

Both of these great theologians put all of the responsibility for salvation on God and none on man. This is called monergism, meaning that all of the work was God's and none was ours, and this was the basis of the protestant reformation and what eighty-five percent of Americans believed when our country was founded. We have strayed from our true belief in the scripture to a lie created by man's reasoning.

24

The lie goes like this: the only way our love for God can be real is if we have free will. Anything less than free will diminishes our capacity for real love. C.S. Lewis, as much as I love most of his writing, was one of the main perpetrators of this false reasoning; yet he said, "I was dragged kicking and screaming into the kingdom of God, eyes darting left and right for some means of escape." Where then was his free will? That sounds like coercion not free will.

What is the truth from God's Word and plain reason? First we have to define free will and if you look at the internet the definitions are endless. However, we will use the definition from the dictionary which says that free will is the "absence of outside constraints." Now to start, we have to see that since we didn't make ourselves, there are some inherent constraints from outside. Psalm 100:3 *Know that the LORD He is God: it is He that has made us, and not we ourselves; we are His people, and the sheep of His pasture.*

We come preprogrammed–as any parent with more than one child can tell you. I have three children and nine grandchildren and they are all different. They were different from birth, so there is some inherent outside constraint. We are limited by our DNA, where we are born, who our parents are and what opportunities we have. These are all outside constraints.

Some say that free will is the ability to choose good or bad, and that without that ability our love would not be real. What about Heaven? When we arrive in Heaven we will no longer have our old sin nature; we will only have our new nature which is the righteousness of Christ. We will have no desire or ability to do wrong, which negates free will, yet our love will be much greater than here because we will have no selfishness.

Stop and think with me for a minute. Is it possible for the infinite God to create a being with a free will? "Of course," you say, "God can do anything." Just a minute, God cannot sin, God cannot go against His nature and the Bible tells us God cannot lie. A lesser God could make a free moral agent, but how can the God Who 'knows the end from the beginning' and controls every energy string of every particle of every atom of every molecule in the universe make something that He does not control? If He knows everything that will ever happen to that being and every thought it will ever have and every action it will ever do before He creates it, how can it be truly free? And if you think that He doesn't know all things, you have created a lesser god.

Notice that I am not saying that we do not have a will; just that it is not free. We have to make decisions every day because we don't know what God has planned. Every decision we make will follow God's perfect will completely. If it follows His revealed will we may be rewarded. If not we will be disciplined.

Many say that the Holy Spirit is a gentleman and never forces Himself on anyone. Once again they are making a god they like, instead of worshipping the true God for Who He is. Let me give you two examples, one from the

Old Testament and one from the New. Incidentally each involves a man named Saul.

The first Saul was king of Israel and, being jealous of David for his popularity, set about to kill him. Saul was told where David was and sent messengers to capture David, but when they came into the company of the prophets the Spirit of God came on them and they started prophesying. He sent more messengers and the same thing happened. Finally Saul came himself and the Spirit came on him and he prophesied also. Did Saul want to prophesy? No, he wanted to kill David. The Holy Spirit controlled him without his permission.

The Saul from the New Testament was also on a mission. He was angry that an imposter had such a popular following and was taking glory from the true God. He was on his way to Damascus to arrest and bring to Jerusalem any who followed this imposter. Suddenly a light from heaven, brighter than the sun, blinded him, and knocked him to the ground. He heard a voice from Heaven saying, *"Saul, Saul, why do you persecute Me?"*

And he said, "Who are You, Lord?" And the Lord said, "I am Jesus whom you persecute: it is hard for you to kick against the pricks."

And he trembling and astonished said, "Lord, what will You have me to do?"

And the Lord said unto him, "Arise, and go into the city, and it shall be told you what you must do." Acts 9:4-6

Is that what Saul wanted? No way! He wanted to get rid of this imposter and his following. Instead he found himself talking to the One he thought was an imposter and finding out he was a chosen vessel of God. Acts 9:15 *But the Lord said unto him (Ananias), "Go your way: for he (Paul) is a chosen vessel unto Me, to bear My name before the Gentiles, and kings, and the children of Israel."* Where was his free will? He was chosen by God to bear His name. No free will here!

> The Bible calls God a "Warrior," a "Despot," "King of kings and Lord of lords" and many other such names, but never a "gentleman."

The Bible never calls God a gentleman; it calls Him a "Warrior," a "Despot," "King of kings and Lord of lords," and many other such names, but never a "gentleman."

I hear some of you saying, "That's not fair, God has to give equal opportunity." That is a ridiculous American idea! God does what He wants to do when He wants to do it. God never claimed to be fair. Fair means treating everyone alike and God has never done that. God is righteous, gracious, merciful, loving, and just, but He is not fair. He doesn't treat everyone alike.

Is it fair that I was born into a strong, loving, Christian family while others are not? Is it fair that most of us are born healthy but many are not? Jesus chose only twelve disciples but spent most of His time with Peter, James, and John? Was that fair? No, but it was right. God always does what is right, but He does not give equal opportunity.

The clearest passage on the sovereignty of God and the bondage of our wills is in Romans 9:15, 16, 18, 21-23 *For He* (God) *said to Moses, "I will have mercy on whom I will have mercy, and I will have compassion on whom I will have compassion." So then it is not of him that wills, nor of him that runs, but of God that shows mercy. Therefore He has mercy on whom He will have mercy, and whom He wills He hardens.*

Has not the potter power over the clay, of the same lump to make one vessel unto honor, and another unto dishonor? What if God, willing to show His wrath, and to make His power known, endured with much longsuffering the vessels of wrath fitted to destruction that He might make known the riches of His glory on the vessels of mercy, which He had before prepared unto glory.

So God shows mercy to whom He wants and hardens whom He wants, and salvation is not by our will or action but by God who shows mercy. God is the Potter and He has the power over us (the clay) to do as He wills, putting up with those He fitted for destruction so that He can show His glory to those of us to whom He chose to show mercy. If this is not your God, then you do not worship the God of the Bible.

John 1:12, 13 *But as many as received Him, to them gave He power to become the sons of God, even to them that believe on His name: which were born, not of blood, nor of the will of the flesh, nor of the will of man, but of God.*

The Bible clearly states that those who have received Jesus were born again by the will of God – not by human will.

"Wait just a minute," you say. "The Bible says that God is not willing that any should perish." Let's take a look at that passage. 2 Peter 3:9 *The Lord is not slack concerning His promise, as some men count slackness; but is longsuffering toward us, not willing that any should perish, but that all should come to repentance.* At first glance it sounds like God wants everyone to go to Heaven, but the Bible also tells us to study not merely read. To whom does the verse say that God is longsuffering? He is longsuffering toward us. Who is 'us'? We find the answer to that in 2 Peter 1:1 *Simon Peter, a servant and an apostle of Jesus Christ, to those that have obtained like precious faith with us through the righteousness of God and our Savior Jesus Christ.* That changes those to whom the 'any' and the 'all' refer. They refer to those who are called to obtain like precious faith. They do not refer to all men as does 1 Timothy 2:3, 4 *For this is good and acceptable in the sight of God our Savior; who will have all men to be saved, and to come to the knowledge of the truth.* Here we have to take a look at the word "will". This is the word "will" denoted in "*Strongs Exhaustive Concordance*" as 2309 meaning inclination, wish or desire whereas the usual word used of God's will is 2307 and denotes determination, choice or decree. (If you don't own a concordance, just enter "Strongs Greek 2309" in a search engine online and you will find the definition.)

The commentary by Albert Barnes says that this word "will" is a desire like God wishing that all men be happy, yet God does many things to make men unhappy for a greater purpose. While saving all men would be enjoyable, it would not accomplish what God has determined. God says He takes no pleasure in the death of the wicked, yet He still kills them and sends them to Hell. Let's take a quick look at some verses that refer to God's pleasure.

Isaiah 46:9, 10 *Remember the former things of old: for I am God, and there is none else; I am God, and there is none like Me, declaring the end from the beginning, and from ancient times the things that are not yet done, saying, My counsel shall stand, and I will do all my pleasure.*

Isaiah 53:10 *Yet it pleased the LORD to bruise Him; He hath put Him to grief: when You shall make His soul an offering for sin, He shall see His seed, He shall prolong His days, and the pleasure of the LORD shall prosper in His hand.*

Luke 12:32 *Fear not, little flock; for it is your Father's good pleasure to give you the kingdom.*

Ephesians 1:5, 6 *Having predestinated us unto the adoption of children by Jesus Christ to Himself, according to the good pleasure of His will, to the praise of the glory of His grace, in which He has made us accepted in the Beloved.*

Philippians 2:13 *For it is God Who works in you <u>both to will and to do of His good pleasure.</u>*

Revelation 4:11 *You are worthy, O Lord, to receive glory and honor and power: for You have created all things, and <u>for Your pleasure they are and were created.</u>*

To sum up, all things exist and were created for God's pleasure, He accomplishes all His pleasure, it pleased God the Father to punish Jesus for our sin, the Father's pleasure will prosper in Jesus' hand (under His control), it is His pleasure to give us the kingdom, He adopted us for His good pleasure and He works in us

> God's perfect will is being completely accomplished exactly as He planned.

to will and to act out His good pleasure. So we do not have a God who is upset or worried about His will not being accomplished, His will is being completely accomplished exactly as He planned. Everyone He has called will come to Him and the rest don't want to come. The <u>only</u> reason we want Him is because He changed us.

Colossians 2:13 *And you, being dead in your sins and the uncircumcision of your flesh, has He made alive together with Him, having forgiven you all trespasses.* <u>While we were dead;</u> what can a dead person do? Stink! And that is all we can do. We cannot believe. We cannot come. We cannot conjure up faith. While we were dead, He made us alive with His life. We now have the life of the Son of God in us. At the point that He makes us alive, we believe, and while we may still have questions, the important things suddenly make sense. We are new creations. We suddenly see the world with new eyes. As the hymn writer, George Robinson wrote:

Heav'n above is softer blue,
Earth around is sweeter green,
Something lives in every hue,
Christless eyes have never seen.
Birds with gladder songs o'erflow,
Flow'rs with deeper beauty shine,
Since I know as now I know,
I am His and He is mine.

Chapter Two

Faith That Triumphs

Many Christians stop at salvation and never move into the joy of victory. They never learn to walk by faith. They never learn to be filled (controlled) by the Holy Spirit. They have their fire insurance and continue to live for themselves. The irony is that people who live for themselves never find true satisfaction or joy. We will never find satisfaction or fulfillment or joy by looking for it. When we learn to walk by faith in what Jesus has already accomplished, we find victory over sin, purpose in life, fulfillment, and joy. Why? Because we are no longer living for ourselves, but for the God who made us; and because of His love we can live for others and learn that real fulfillment comes from loving and serving God and loving and serving others.

> The irony is that people who live for themselves never find true satisfaction or joy.

We cannot live for others in our own strength; we need to be filled with the Holy Spirit. How do we do that? We need to: ask for Him to fill us, yield to His guidance, and depend on Him for all that we say and do. As soon as we go our own way we will cease being filled. Obedience is the key to maintaining the filling. We will not always be filled but as believers we will always be indwelt by the Spirit.

Understanding Forgiveness

God has given us everything we need to live a victorious life, but we need to know the weapons to take hold of that victory. The first one we need to know and understand is that we are forgiven, completely and totally. This is very important because if we think God is angry with us for our sin we will stay away from Him and stay in our sin. I was addicted to pornography until I was 33 years old. I felt that God was at least disappointed in me and at worst angry with me. I wanted to stay away from God until He cooled off, which kept me in the sin longer. Stupid, but all of Satan's lies are.

I have asked many believers if they understand their forgiveness in Christ. They almost always answer in the affirmative, but when I hear them pray they are still asking God for forgiveness. That shows me that they really don't understand that they have been forgiven.

How many of you have been taught that God will forgive you when you confess your sin or when you forgive others? Let's take a look at the scripture passages that are used to make these arguments.

Matthew 6:14, 15 states: *"For if you forgive men their trespasses, your heavenly Father will also forgive you: But if you forgive not men their trespasses, neither will your Father forgive your trespasses."* Now this seems cut and dried, and since Jesus Himself said it, it must be true; yet if it is true today, it makes a stark contradiction with

Ephesians 4:32 *"And be kind one to another, tenderhearted, forgiving one another, even as God for Christ's sake has forgiven you."* These are opposites; the one clearly states that we won't be forgiven unless we forgive, while the other just as clearly states that we should forgive because we have been forgiven. Some would say that Jesus teaching takes precedence as He is God, but they do not understand that Jesus did everything while He was on earth through the power of the Holy Spirit, just as Paul wrote the book of Ephesians by the power of that same Spirit, making both verses equally from God. Both verses are absolutely true in the time frames in which they were applicable.

God tells us through Paul in 2 Timothy 2:15 *"Study to show yourself approved unto God, a workman that needs not to be ashamed, rightly dividing the word of truth."* What does it mean to rightly divide the word of truth? It means to divide the times in which things were written as well as to whom it was written. Not everything in the Bible applies directly to us. For instance, in Exodus the Israelites were told not to eat unclean animals, yet 1 Timothy 4:4, 5 says *"For every creature of God is good, and nothing is to be refused, if it is received with thanksgiving: for it is sanctified by the word of God and prayer."* Obviously we are not under the law today but are free to eat what we choose, thanking God for it. Here we have rightly divided the Word of truth.

How can we rightly divide the verses on forgiveness? What great event divides them? The greatest event in history–the cross–divides them! Before the cross no one could be totally forgiven. That is why believers who died could not go to Heaven but were kept in paradise until the cross. Hebrews 10:4 *For it is not possible that the blood of bulls and of goats should take away sins.* The sacrifices of the Old Testament only pushed the sin back; they could not get rid of it. Jesus' blood, however, paid the price for the sin of the whole world; past, present, and future. It is because of His death on the cross that we who are in Christ stand completely forgiven. Do you need more verses to convince you? Here are a few:

Ephesians 1:5-7 *Having predestinated us unto the adoption of sons by Jesus Christ to Himself, according to the good pleasure of His will, To the praise of the glory of His grace, in which He has made us accepted in the Beloved. In Whom we <u>have</u> redemption through His blood, the <u>forgiveness</u> of sins, according to the riches of His grace.*

Colossians 1:13, 14 *Who has delivered us from the power of darkness, and has translated us into the kingdom of His dear Son: In Whom we <u>have</u> redemption through His blood, even the <u>forgiveness</u> of sins.*

Colossians 2:13 *And you, being dead in your sins and the uncircumcision of your flesh, has He quickened together with Him, <u>having forgiven you all trespasses.</u>*

Notice especially that last one. Having forgiven is the past perfect tense. That means it is an action completed in the past with ongoing results, and it was completed when Jesus said "It is finished" while He was hanging on the cross. Also notice that it says all trespasses. That is why there is <u>NO</u> condemnation to those who are in Christ Jesus. All trespasses means all: past, present, and future.

There is one more verse that believers always bring up that sounds like our forgiveness is conditional. It's a great verse, but it doesn't mean what they think it means–it means much more. 1 John 1:9 says: *"If we confess our sin, He is faithful and just to forgive us our sins and to cleanse us from all unrighteousness."* If we take the English version at face value it certainly sounds like we are forgiven after we confess our sin, but if we look at the original Greek, the word that is translated "forgive" is *aphiemi* (*Strong's Concordance* number 863). It certainly can be translated "forgive", but it is the same word used in 1 Corinthians 7:11 which is translated "put away" or "divorce". Now if we know from the previous passages that we are already forgiven all of our sins, past, present, and future; we know that this word cannot mean "forgiven". It must mean "put away" or "divorce". Suddenly it all makes sense and it fits better with the context, which is not forgiveness but walking in the light, or victory in the Christian life.

"If we confess our sins" means: if we agree with God about our sins. We must learn to hate our sin as God does and say the same thing that He does about it. We do this by looking at the verses in the Bible that call it sin, memorizing them, and by looking at the consequences of our sin if it is carried out to its logical conclusion.

I had to look at the consequences of pornography if I kept viewing it. My children and all others under my ministry would be less protected from sexual temptations; I would eventually commit adultery or worse: rape or molestation. I would lose my family, my ministry, my freedom, and possibly my life as all serial killers started with pornography and none of them planned on becoming serial killers when they started.

> Sin will always hurt us and those we love; don't ever forget that.

An unknown author penned the following words: "Sin will always take you farther than you wanted to go, sin will always keep you longer than you wanted to stay and sin will always cost you more than you wanted to pay." Sin will always hurt us and those we love; don't ever forget that.

Confessing means we need to call sin by the same name God does, to admit that we did it, to admit it is as bad as He says it is, and to use the weapons He has put at our disposal to conquer it. God says that *He is faithful and just to divorce us from our sin"* which means when we confess our sin, He will take the sin out of our lives. When we really learn to hate our sin as God does we won't be tempted by that sin anymore unless we are tricked into changing our minds again. For years I had a love-hate relationship with pornography. I loved it before and during my sin and hated it afterward.

I could stay away from it for two or three months on my own strength, but I would always fall. I asked God many times to take away my desire for pornography, but He never did until I learned what 1 John 1:9 really meant and put it to work in my life. By God's grace I have not viewed pornography for over twenty-five years. All of the credit, of course, goes to God.

The last part of the verse says, *"And to cleanse us from all unrighteousness."* God will keep working on the other sins in our lives until we come to the place that we agree with Him about those sins as well, so He can divorce us from them also. We will not run out of sin before we get to Heaven, but we can live much more victoriously than we do now.

Some people say, "If I can't be perfect, what's the use?"

I ask them, "What is the perfect time in which to run the mile?"

They usually answer with something in the high three-minute range. But the right answer is zero seconds! Jesus can do it! Why then do people constantly train to run the mile if they can never achieve perfection? Because they want to win the prize. 1 Corinthians 9:24 *"Don't you know that they which run in a race all run, but one receives the prize? So run, that you may obtain."* We are to keep pressing on to win the *"prize of the high calling of God in Christ Jesus."*

If you have put your faith in Jesus Christ, you are totally forgiven for all of your sin–past, present and future. The Father will never be angry with you for anything. He took out his anger on His own Son as Jesus became sin for us. 2 Corinthians 5:20, 21 *Now then we are ambassadors for Christ, as though God did beseech you by us: we pray you in Christ's stead, be reconciled to God. For He has made Him to be sin for us, Who knew no sin; that we might be made the righteousness of God in Him.* The sinless Son of God became my sin and your sin so that we could have His righteousness.

1 John 4:10 *Herein is love, not that we loved God, but that He loved us, and sent his Son to be the propitiation for our sins.* A propitiation is a payment to satisfy the anger of the one who has been wronged. We sin against God, Who hates sin, and Jesus was the payment that satisfied His wrath. Our Heavenly Father will never be angry with us because He spent His anger on Jesus and we are now the righteousness of Christ. Every time God looks at you and me He sees Jesus' righteousness.

Some would say that God can't even remember our sin, but that is ridiculous. He will never remember our sin against us, but He knows all and doesn't forget why He is disciplining us, or wonder what we are talking about when we confess our sin.

Others say that total forgiveness is a dangerous teaching because believers will take advantage of God's forgiveness and continue to sin. I say that if God did not want us to understand His complete forgiveness, He wouldn't have put these verses in His Word. If a believer continues to sin, God promises to discipline those He

> If you can sin and get away with it, you had better check your salvation!

loves, so if you can sin and get away with it, you had better check your salvation! Hebrews 12:6 *For whom the Lord loves He chastens, and scourges every son whom*

He receives. All believers are disciplined for their sin, but not punished, as Jesus took all of our punishment. The difference is the outlook. Punishment looks back; it is payment for having done something wrong. Discipline looks forward to the finished product–making us a disciple. Total forgiveness is the truth, and it is one of the necessary weapons in the battle against sin.

Christian cults will not teach total forgiveness because they want to control people. We want to set them free by having the Holy Spirit to control them. We want to educate believers so they can keep short accounts with God, and desire to be close to Him because of His great forgiveness and love.

If you adopted a child from an orphanage, he would believe that staying with you would be based on his performance. Is that how you want him to feel? Or do you want your child to rest in your unconditional love? God wants us to rest in His unconditional love and not worry about losing our salvation. He loves us with the same love with which He loved Jesus before the world began and He will never change His mind.

Being dead to sin.
The next weapon in our arsenal is the fact that we are dead to sin. Notice that it is a fact in Romans 6:1-3 *What shall we say then? Shall we continue in sin, that grace may abound? God forbid. How shall we, that <u>are dead to sin</u>, live any longer in it? Don't you know that all of us who were baptized into Jesus Christ were baptized into His death?* If we have been baptized into Jesus Christ, which happens at the new birth, we are dead to sin. When

we put our faith in Jesus, the Holy Spirit baptizes us into the body of Christ. Romans 12:5 *So we, being many, are* <u>*one body*</u> *in Christ, and every one members one of another.* 1 Corinthians 12:13,27 *For by one Spirit are we all* <u>*baptized into one body*</u>*, whether we are Jews or Gentiles, whether we are bond or free; and have been all made to drink into one Spirit. Now you are the body of Christ, and members in particular.*

So all of us who are believers were baptized into Jesus Christ and are therefore dead to sin. What does that mean? I certainly don't always feel dead to sin.

It means that our old man or old nature was crucified on the cross with Christ and no longer controls us; and for the first time we have the possibility of doing the right thing through our new nature, which is as righteous as Jesus Christ Himself.

When we believe the facts that God says are true concerning any temptation, we will not fall to that temptation. Does this really work? Absolutely! It works on the very same principle on which our salvation works. What God accomplished on the cross is true for us whether or not we believe it. If we do not believe it, it does us no good. If we do believe it, it makes all the difference in the world.

I remember one of the guys from a sexual addictions accountability group, where we had been memorizing Romans chapter 6, coming in one week saying, "It works! It really works!"

I asked, "What works?"

He replied, "That thing about being dead to sin. My wife was visiting relatives this weekend and I thought about trying to get past the filter on my computer. The thought came to me, "You're dead to that;" so I said it out loud and the desire went away."

Paul tells us in Romans 6:11 *Count yourselves to be dead indeed unto sin, but alive unto God through Jesus Christ our Lord.* We need to actively count, reckon or believe (depending on your translation) that we are dead to sin. Romans 7:20 says, *"Now if I do that which I do not desire, it is no more I that do it, but sin that lives in me."* In other words, we need to believe that we <u>are</u> our new nature and that our old nature is dead, because that is exactly what God says is the truth. Jesus said, *"If you continue in my word, then are you my disciples indeed, and you shall know the truth, and the truth shall make you free."* John 8:31, 32. If you want to be free, you must know the truth, believe it, and act accordingly.

> If you want to be free, you must know the truth, believe it, and act accordingly.

I do not believe we have the desire or capacity, while we are in these bodies, to believe God about every temptation; so we will not achieve perfection in this life. I do, however, believe that through the Spirit we can cultivate our desire to be like Jesus and love Him more and have complete victory over specific sins in our lives. It really does work and it is how God shows His power in us.

Accountability
Without serious, loving accountability we are still doomed to failure. Why? Because we are <u>still</u> human, but we are not <u>only</u> human. Every time someone says, "Well I'm only human," I reply, "I can tell you how to be saved." That usually surprises them enough to get their attention.

Then I point them to 2 Peter 1:3 *According as His divine power has given to us all things that pertain unto life and godliness, through the knowledge of Him that has called us to glory and virtue: by which are given unto us exceeding great and precious promises: that by these you might be <u>partakers of the divine nature</u>, having escaped the corruption that is in the world through lust.* We are partakers of the divine nature (a better translation of "*you might be partakers*" is "*you become partakers*"). Our new nature is the righteousness of Jesus Christ. We will never become gods like some cults teach, but we have God's nature. He is our Father and we should be acting like Him because we have His DNA.

The problem is that we still have our old nature until we die; so we are still human and God has designed us to live in community and with accountability. The American icon is the rugged individual who always comes through with the rescue and always gets his girl.

We have an amazing negative example of this in Elijah. He is the consummate individualist. He single-handedly takes on 450 prophets of Baal, challenges them to a duel of sacrifices, taunts them, beats them hands down and then has them all killed. Through his prayer the rain is held back for three and a half years, fire comes from heaven and burns up a water-soaked sacrifice, Israel is turned back to God, the rain returns, and Elijah outruns King Ahab's chariot. What a man's man!

Then what happens? Elijah gets a note from Queen Jezebel saying that he would soon lose his head; so what does he do? He loses his head, forgets that his God does miracles, and runs away. What is the problem? He thinks he's alone. There's no one to remind or encourage him. Whose fault is it? Elijah's. Obadiah has a hundred prophets hidden in a cave. There are over seven thousand men in Israel who have never bowed the knee to Baal.

Does Elijah know any of them? No, he was a loner, and that is why he ran away. Ultimately that is one reason that Elijah's ministry ends on a sour note. Elijah wants to die, but God sends him first to anoint Elisha to take over his ministry.

Elisha is much more relational than Elijah. He spends a lot of time with the other prophets and has a relationship with a family. I believe that is part of the reason that fourteen miracles are recorded in Elisha's ministry while only seven are recorded in Elijah's. The other reason, of course, is that Elisha asked for a double portion of Elijah's spirit. If you are checking this out–and I really hope you check everything I write with scripture–you will find the fourteenth miracle in 2 Kings 13:21. It happens after Elisha's death to show that the power is from God, not Elisha.

We are designed to have friends who will really hold us accountable so that we have a steady growth in our life as followers of Jesus, instead of the roller coaster ride to which most of us have become accustomed. It is so easy for us to grow hot and cold over and over or, worse yet, become lukewarm and stay there. I never want to be without accountability partners because I want to finish well and not have any major failures on the way. Why? Because I want to glorify my Master and I want to be able to say to those I mentor, "Follow me as I follow Christ." If you can't say that, you're not in the battle. We need to be in the battle, not just for us but for the next generation. If you can't tell me what sins you are battling, you're not in the battle. If you don't have accountability partners you're not in the battle. If we're not in the battle we're wasting oxygen.

> I never want to be without accountability partners because I want to finish well.

When you look for an accountability partner, don't look for someone that you can intimidate. If you are a pastor, it may be best to find another pastor because most of your congregation will be afraid to really ask the hard questions; and often those who aren't afraid may not have your best interest in mind. We all need to look for a mature, on-fire believer who really wants to glorify God and who wants to be held accountable as well.

Many Christians refuse to be held accountable because they are afraid to share with anyone who they really are or what their struggles are. We are told in James 5:16 *Confess your faults one to another, and pray one for another, that you may be healed.* We are as sick as our deepest secret. When we share who we are with God (Who knows us better than we do) and with another person, we start the healing process.

One of the biggest problems we have in most churches is that they are full of hypocrites. That is what the world claims, and sadly it is true. Most believers come to church playing the part of being what they think a Christian should be. They pretend to be good and when an unbeliever comes there are two basic reactions: one is, "I could never be that good so I won't come back," or two, "I know them and they're not that good, I don't want to be a hypocrite so I don't belong."

> If we as believers can't be real, we will never win people to Jesus.

If we as believers can't be real, we will never win people to Jesus. Why is it so hard to be real? It's because of our pride. We want people to think we are better than we are, so we hide and stay in bondage instead of throwing away our pride and becoming truly free in Christ. I heard a story as a small boy that resonated with me.

It seems Mary and Bobby were sent to visit Grandma and Grandpa on the farm. When they arrived, Grandma gave a present to Mary, and Grandpa gave one to Bobby. Mary opened hers finding a lovely doll which she adored. Bobby received a slingshot and was very excited to try it out. With a warning not to hit any animals, he ran outside to the nearby woods.

Bobby tried and tried to hit trees or rocks with the stones he found, but the stones always curved away from the target. Discouraged, Bobby headed home. When he was almost back to the house he saw Grandma's prize goose and took a shot knowing he couldn't hit it. To his surprise and dismay the stone flew true and struck the goose in the head and it dropped in its tracks. Now Bobby was afraid. He looked around to see if anyone was watching. Seeing no one, Bobby dragged the heavy goose to the woodpile and covered it with pieces of wood.

As Bobby walked back to the house, Mary popped out from behind the garden shed. "I saw what you did!" she whispered. "If you do my chores, I won't tell Grandma."

Bobby was horrified, but he felt he had no choice. "Ok," he muttered.

After dinner Grandma asked Mary to help with the dishes. "Oh Grandma, Bobby wants to do the dishes, don't you Bobby?" Mary asked.

"Yeah, I do," Bobby replied feigning enthusiasm.

The next morning Grandma asked Mary to help fold the clothes, and again, Mary made Bobby do it. This continued the rest of that day and into the next. By the afternoon of the third day, Bobby had had enough. He went to Grandma with tears in his eyes and confessed about her favorite goose. "I really didn't mean to do it," Bobby cried, "I'm so sorry!"

"I knew you did it, I saw you from the kitchen window," Grandma said, "I wondered how long you would be Mary's slave."

"If you saw me why didn't you say anything?" asked Bobby.

"You needed to see how guilt makes you a slave and confession sets you free," Grandma answered.

> "You needed to see how guilt makes you a slave and confession sets you free."

"It does feel good to be free," sighed Bobby happily.

After dinner, Grandma asked Mary to help with the dishes. Mary tried her usual way to get Bobby to do them, but Bobby retorted, "I think it's your turn."

Surprised, she whispered, "I'll tell Grandma!"

"I already did," Bobby laughed, "You're not my boss anymore!"

I found that freedom in 1985 when I confessed my sin of pornography to the whole church; I was truly free. I was no longer afraid that someone would find out, and because of my confession, other guys started coming to me for help to be set free. It is almost impossible to be set free until we confess our sin to another human being.

Do not confuse accountability with legalism. Accountability is voluntary and sets us free. Legalism is forced, either by others, or by our misunderstanding of scripture, and makes us slaves. Legalism comes in three types.

1. If we believe that sinning will keep us and others from Heaven; that is legalism because it becomes a works salvation.

2. If we believe that doing or not doing a certain thing, makes us more attractive to God; that is legalism.

3. If we try to make others do or not do a certain thing which is not specifically called sin in the scripture, that is legalism.

Let me give you an example. If I tell you that you have to keep the Sabbath to please God, I am being legalistic. "Wait a minute," you say, "breaking the Sabbath is specifically called sin in the scripture." Yes, but to whom was the law given? Exodus 19:5 tells us: *Now therefore, if you (Israel) will obey My voice indeed, and keep My covenant, then you shall be a peculiar treasure unto Me above all people: for all the earth is Mine.* God specifically tells us that He gave His law to Israel to set them above all other peoples.

Exodus 31:12-17 *And the LORD spoke unto Moses, saying, Speak also unto the children of Israel, saying, "Truly My Sabbaths you shall keep: for they are a sign between Me and you throughout your generations; that you may know that I am the LORD that sanctifies you. You shall keep the Sabbath therefore; for it is holy unto you: every one that defiles it shall surely be put to death: for whoever does any work therein, that soul shall be cut off from among his people. Six days may work be done; but in the seventh is the Sabbath of rest, holy to the LORD: whoever does any work in the Sabbath day, he shall surely be put to death.*

Wherefore the children of Israel shall keep the Sabbath, to observe the Sabbath throughout their generations, for a perpetual covenant. It is a sign between Me and the children of Israel for ever: for in six days the LORD made heaven and earth, and on the seventh day He rested, and was refreshed.

The Sabbath law was never given to the Gentiles, but was given to the people of Israel alone. Paul tells us not to let anyone judge us in regard to the Sabbath in Colossians 2:16, 17 *Let no man therefore judge you in meat, or in drink, or in respect of an holyday, or of the new moon, or of the Sabbath days: Which are a shadow of things to come; but the body is of Christ.* Paul is saying don't go back to the shadow when you have the substance.

Is it wrong to keep the Sabbath? No. Not if you do it for the right reason. Paul says in Romans 14:5, 6 *One man regards one day above another: another regards every day alike. Let every man be fully persuaded in his own mind. He that regards the day, regards it unto the Lord; and he that regards not the day, to the Lord he does not regard it.* The point is: why am I doing what I am doing? Is it for God's glory or for mine?

So we always need to be careful what we tell others they must or must not do and why. Legalism always enslaves and we need to be careful that accountability does not turn into legalism. Accountability done for the glory of God will always set us free. The following verses put it all in perspective:

1 Corinthians 10:31 *Whether therefore you eat, or drink, or whatever you do, do all to the glory of God.*

Colossians 3:17 *And whatever you do in word or deed, do all in the Name of the Lord Jesus, giving thanks to God and the Father by Him.*

Eating and drinking are pretty mundane things yet God wants all the glory in everything we do. In fact, if we are doing anything that does not glorify God we need to stop, and we need accountability to do that because it is so easy to change our minds when the temptation comes. I wish that my first thought was always about Jesus when I am tempted, but often it is, "If I do this, I'll have to tell the guys in my group." That may not be the best reason, but it helps me resist temptation, and that is a good thing.

I want to close this section with an old story which I believe perfectly illustrates the difference between doing the right thing under the law, and living free under grace.

There was a woman who was married to a drunk who would often beat her if she didn't do everything the way he liked it done. One day he wrote out a list of things for her to do every day and told her that if she did not do all of it every day, he would beat her. She hated this list, but because her fear kept her from leaving him, she tried very hard every day to accomplish it each day, so she wouldn't be beaten. One day her husband was killed in a bar fight and, of course, she was relieved.

Some years later she fell in love with a wonderful Christian man and not long after, they were married. She was so thrilled to be truly loved, cherished, and respected the way a wife should be. As she was going through some papers one day, she ran across the list her former husband had given her. She was amazed as she looked over the list which she had so hated in the past, that she did all of these tasks every day without even thinking about it. She was so much in love that they had become a part of her daily routine without even trying.

This is exactly the way we should be living our lives. We should be so much in love with Jesus that we are excited about doing the things He would like us to do, and not doing the things that He doesn't want us to do.

Chapter Three

Faith That Calms

We started in chapter one with "How to have peace <u>with</u> God." Now we are looking at "How to have the peace <u>of</u> God," or how to have complete peace regardless of the circumstances because God is in control, and He loves us. To have the peace of God in our lives we need to know that we can trust Him completely.

What do I need to know about another person before I can trust him? If I were climbing a rock wall and had a spotter on the other end of the rope for my safety, I need to trust the spotter or I won't climb the wall. What do I need to know about this spotter before I can trust him? What do I need to know about God before I can trust Him? God asks us to trust Him enough that we will come to Him and grow in our relationship with Him and learn to trust Him in every circumstance, but how can we do that? There are three things that I need to know about my spotter and about God before I can trust them.

Does God care enough?
The first thing I need to know is that He cares enough about me to keep me safe. Of course there is a huge difference between trusting God for my whole being for

all eternity and trusting someone to keep me safe on a rock wall, but the principles are the same. If I think that when a pretty girl comes along my climbing spotter will watch her instead of watching me and taking care of his end of the rope, I am not going up the wall.

Does God care enough about us so that we can trust Him with our body, soul, and spirit for eternity? Absolutely! And here's the proof: John 3:16 *For God so loved the world that He gave his only begotten Son, that whoever believes in Him should not perish, but have everlasting life.* Romans 8:32 *He that spared not His own Son, but delivered Him up for us all, how shall He not with Him also freely give us all things?* God loves you and me enough that He gave Jesus, His only Son so that we can be with Him forever and He will give us all things. And Jesus said in John 15:13 *Greater love has no man than this, that a man lay down his life for his friends.* And since God cannot change, (Malachi 3:6 *For I am the LORD, I change not.)* He will never change in His love for us. God, the Father loves us with exactly the same love that He loves Jesus Christ. John 17:23 *I in them, and You in Me, that they may be made perfect in one; and that the world may know that You have sent Me, and have loved them, as You have loved Me.* That little word "as" should be translated "just as" or "in the same way". So, one of the criteria is taken care of for us to be able to trust Him; He loves us far beyond our understanding.

> God loves us far beyond our understanding.

Is God strong enough?
The second criteria we need to know about a person is his strength. There are many older ladies in our church who love me, but I would not put my trust in them as a spotter for my rock wall climb because they do not have the strength. I want someone who is greater and stronger so that if I fall, I will not be hurt. The question then is: can we know that God has enough power to take care of us?

John 1:3 *All things were made by Him (Jesus); and without Him was not any thing made that was made.*

Matthew 19:26 *But Jesus beheld them, and said unto them, "With men this is impossible; but with God all things are possible."* Since Jesus created all things, and nothing is impossible for Him, He has awesome power.

This book cannot prove creation to you, but I want to give you one easily-understood example of why macro-evolution could never happen. It is the law of irreducible complexity. That may sound intimidating but it is easily illustrated with a mousetrap. Each part of the mouse trap is essential for the trap to work. If we take away the smallest part—one staple, for example—it will never catch a mouse; it cannot even be set. In the same way, most cells in living things are irreducibly complex. If we take away any part, the cell will die. This means that all the parts of a cell had to evolve at the same time, be put together, and somehow be given life.

If you take all the parts of a mouse trap and put them in a clothes dryer, how long would it take for them to come together to form a mouse trap? And then, to be fair, it would have to set itself, which would correspond to giving itself life. Yet, this example is still not nearly as complex as the pieces of a cell coming together because there are fewer parts, and we supplied the parts and the clothes dryer. Macro-evolution is clearly impossible.

The correct interpretation of the Bible and true science will always agree. That is because God is the author of both. Many Christians fall into the trap of believing that the Bible claims that the universe is less than ten thousand years old. Don't misunderstand, I believe that God could have created the world in an instant if He had desired, but if your mind is open enough, you will find that there is plenty of evidence for an old universe that started from a point and is still expanding today.

One of the arguments of the "young earth scientists" is from a verse in Romans that says "*death came by sin*." And they assume that this is referring to the death of all life, not just human life, which is a ridiculous argument. Plants die and since God told Adam that he could eat from every tree in the garden, that means they ate fruit and that fruit had to die. According to scripture a seed cannot grow unless it dies and digestion involves the death of bacteria. So the "*death came by sin*" is not referring to anything but human death.

Without death the flies could have taken over the whole world. The following is a quote from SCAPest.com:

"To give an idea as to how rapidly flies can propagate, according to entomologist Hodges, 'A pair of flies beginning operations in April may be progenitors, if all were to live, of 191,010,000,000,000,000,000, flies by August. Allowing 1/8 of a cubic inch to each fly, this number would cover the earth 47 feet deep.'"

I believe that this gives enough evidence that there was death before sin, but not human death. Man was made in the image of God; the animals were not, and to use this verse on which to base a theory of a young creation is wrong and, from a human point of view excludes most scientists from Christianity. There are many proofs of an old creation like red shift, magnetic pole shift, age of stars, and star clusters, but that is not the purpose of this book.

My main point is that God did create the universe just as He claims: by His spoken word. There is a scientific theory, which I believe is correct, called "string theory." It theorizes that each part of the atom is made up of billions of strings of energy. God turned some of His power into matter by His spoken word and He sustains it by the word of His power. Hebrews 1:3 *Who, being the brightness of his glory, and the express image of his person, and upholding all things by the word of his power, when he had by Himself purged our sins, sat down on the right hand of the Majesty on high.*

We have seen the power of nuclear explosions, where a small amount of matter becomes a great amount of energy or power. When God created matter it took that same amount of power to make the small amount of matter of which the bomb was made. We have all heard the equation: $E=mc^2$. Simply put, this means energy is equal to mass times the speed of light squared. More simply, it takes a whole lot of power to make a tiny bit of matter, yet our universe is huge beyond our understanding. That means that our God used an unimaginably enormous amount of power when He made the universe, yet He lost no power doing it because by definition His power is infinite. Remember that God's power is separate from Him so that matter is not God. Animistic religions would say that God is in everything. God is everywhere present but is not in His creation, except in His indwelling of us. Power is something God has and controls. Since God's power is infinite, we have the second criteria we need to trust Him.

Is God wise enough?
The third and final thing we need to know about a person to know if we can trust him is that he is wise enough to do the right thing in every situation. There is a man in our church who loves me and is a huge strong man, but God has not given him the wisdom he would need to be my spotter for the rock wall climb. Wisdom is the right use of knowledge. How much does God know and how wise is He? Read Job, chapters 38-41 to see a little of God's understanding of nature. Here are a few verses on God's wisdom.

Proverbs 3:19 *The LORD by wisdom hath founded the earth; by understanding has he established the heavens.*

Colossians 2:3 *In Whom (Christ) are hid all the treasures of wisdom and knowledge.*

1Timothy 1:17 *Now unto the King eternal, immortal, invisible, the only wise God, be honor and glory for ever and ever. Amen.*

Jude 1:25 *To the only wise God our Savior, be glory and majesty, dominion and power, both now and ever. Amen.*

Romans 11:33 *O the depth of the riches both of the wisdom and knowledge of God! How unsearchable are His judgments, and His ways past finding out!*

When we look at nature and all of its balances, ingenuity, and imagination; and look at the scripture and see the way God has revealed Himself to us: we can know beyond a shadow of a doubt that God's wisdom is infinite. Psalm 139:2 *You know my downsitting and my uprising, You understand my thoughts afar off.* He knows us individually, minutely, and completely. He knows every thought we have ever had or ever will have.

We can trust God completely, in every situation, because he loves us completely, is all-powerful, and He has all wisdom and knowledge.

The problem of evil
So where does evil fit in? If God is completely trustworthy because of His love, power, and wisdom; why do bad things happen to His kids? Most Christians would say that through the free will they say was given to Lucifer, who became Satan, and later the free will they say was given to man, evil came into the world; but what does the Bible really say? I want God's knowledge, not man's opinion.

We will start with a verse that is quite well-known to most Christians, but most either do not understand or do not believe it. Romans 8:28 "And *we know that all things*

63

work together for <u>good</u> to those who love God, to those who are the <u>called</u> according to <u>His purpose</u>." The verse starts with "and we know," showing that this is a fact–something that is true whether or not we believe it.

The next thing we notice is that little three-letter word "all". Many have heard the saying that, "all means all and that's all all means." While that is not always true, it is true in this case. "All things" includes everything, good and bad, that has happened and ever will happen to us who are believers. We'll come back to this verse later in the chapter.

There is an email going around that deals with the problem of evil, which basically comes up with an answer that evil is the absence of God and really not a "thing" since God created all things and could not create evil. Try telling someone who has been raped, or just received word that a loved one was killed by a drunk driver, that nothing happened; it was just the absence of God. It sounds more like Christian Science than real Christianity. They say that evil does not exist and we just need to keep confessing that it does not exist and it will go away. That of course is neither Christian nor science. Evil is something real, it is a real entity which Christ has conquered, but has yet to be wiped out.

There is an old joke about a Baptist, a Catholic, and a Christian Science follower who all wind up in Hell. The Baptist says, "I blew it, I'm stuck here."

The Catholic says, "I'm not too worried, I've got someone praying me out of here."

The Christian Scientist says, "I'm not here!"

The problem of evil is the greatest obstacle mentioned by unbelievers that keeps them from becoming believers. Most believers struggle with this as well. How can a good God allow so much evil to exist in the world? First, we need to define evil.

If the laws of God come from His character, then evil must be the opposite of His character. It is man in his pride doing what he wants to do. Yet that does not cover everything. Is a hurricane evil? How about an earthquake and tsunami? These are not evil in the same sense as a rape or murder, yet they can cause just as much hurt. How much of this does God control? What is evil?

Proverbs 8:13 *The fear of the LORD is to <u>hate evil</u>: pride, and arrogancy, and the evil way, and the perverse mouth, do I hate.*

Does God hate sin? Absolutely, one hundred percent **YES!** Has God ever committed sin? Absolutely, one hundred percent **NO!** If we are to properly fear and please God, we will hate sin, but we must not just hate the sin in others, but in <u>our</u> old nature as well.

Does God have a purpose for evil? Obviously He does. Whether we're talking about natural disasters and catastrophes, sickness, and disease, or moral evil that God calls sin, God has good purposes in evil. For instance, God wants all of His creation to see His manifold, or many splendored, or multi-faceted wisdom.

That is why He created all things, and especially the Church. Without evil, God could not show His justice, mercy or grace. Have you stopped to think how much less you would appreciate God if there were no evil? Much of what we love about God is his grace, mercy, and justice.

Ephesians 3:9, 10 *And to make all see what is the fellowship of the mystery, which from the beginning of the world has been hid in God, Who created all things by Jesus Christ: to the intent that now unto the principalities and powers in heavenly places might be known by the church the manifold wisdom of God.* God wants us to know Him more experientially because He knows that the better we know Him the better off we will be. He is showing the angels, good and fallen, Who He is by His dealings with us.

Did God create evil? This is still one of the more hotly-debated issues in Christendom. Most theologians do gymnastics on the scriptures that would astound Olympic judges to keep from saying that God could have created evil, thinking that if God created evil, He is evil–and nothing could be further from the truth. God can do many things without sinning which, if we did them, would be sin for us.

If I kill someone, or physically harm someone who is not harming me or harming another person, that is sin. God ends thousands of people's lives every day without sin. He takes credit for making people deaf and blind. Exodus 4:11 *And the LORD said unto him, "Who made man's mouth? or who makes the mute, or the deaf, or the seeing, or the blind? Have not I the LORD?"* God can do anything that is according to His nature without sinning. The only thing that could be sin for God is to go against His nature. Is it against His nature to create an enemy for Him to fight and subdue in order to show His strength?

Why did God raise Pharaoh to power? God gives the answer to Moses to tell Pharaoh in Exodus 9:16 *And in very deed for this cause have I raised you up, <u>to show in you My power</u>; and that My Name may be declared throughout all the earth.* If God can raise up a man to great power to oppose Him so that He can show how great He is, why cannot God create evil as the ultimate opponent, "embodied" in Satan, whom God created as Lucifer.

Did God know that Lucifer would become Satan before He created him? Of course; God knows the end from the beginning. Isaiah 46:9, 10 *Remember the former things of old: for I am God, and there is none else; I am God, and there is none like me, <u>declaring the end from the beginning</u>, and from ancient times the things that are not yet done, saying, My counsel shall stand, and I will do all My pleasure.*

He knows all: Colossians 2:3 *In whom (Christ) are hid all the treasures of wisdom and knowledge.*

Romans 11:33 *O the depth of the riches both of the wisdom and knowledge of God! How unsearchable are His judgments, and His ways past finding out!*

God created Lucifer
knowing every detail
of what would happen
for all eternity.

God created Lucifer knowing every detail of what would happen for all eternity. God has a good purpose for evil and He created it for that good purpose. Isaiah 45:7 *"I form the light, and create darkness: I make peace, and create evil: I the LORD do all these things."* This is one of the verses that most theologians are doing such amazing gymnastics to get around, that they hurt themselves. I was taught in Bible school, "If the plain sense makes good sense, seek no other sense." Personally I would change that to: don't try to replace it with another sense, because many of the true stories of the Bible are also allegories–but we will deal with those later.

It is obvious to me that God is talking about all of the types of evil described above, because He said He created darkness. Physical darkness is the absence of light, and in my limited understanding of science, it did not have to be created. 2 Corinthians 4:6 *"For God, who commanded the light to shine out of darkness, has shined in our hearts, to give the light of the knowledge of the glory of God in the face of Jesus Christ."* Therefore He must be referring in this verse in Isaiah to moral and spiritual darkness, which is equivalent to with moral and spiritual evil.

In the context of this verse, God refers to the gods of the nations and compares Himself to them, though He is incomparable. These gods were gods of specific things like fertility, rain, and sun. Some were considered good and some were evil; all had to be appeased. God is saying, 'I am incomparable, I made everything, good and bad for My purpose and I control everything for My purpose.

Paul, in his ecstatic adulation of God in Romans 11 finishes with: "*For of Him, and through Him, and to Him, are all things: to Whom be glory for ever. Amen.*" God takes credit for having created all things. "Of", "to" and "through" are very interesting words meaning that God created and sustains all things for His purposes and glory. If that does not include evil, we need to change the Bible.

It is even more specific when Paul says in Colossians 1:16 *For by Him were all things created, that are in heaven, and that are in earth, visible and invisible, whether they be thrones, or dominions, or principalities, or powers: all things were created by Him, and for Him.*

Paul, by the Holy Spirit, is not just talking about physical governments, but about spiritual powers as in angels good and evil. Our amazing God takes the responsibility and the glory for the creation of good and evil, and the control of all things good and evil, yet never takes away the responsibility of man. He holds man completely responsible for his sin.

Let me give you an example from King David's life about God's control and David's responsibility. 2 Samuel 24:1 *And again the anger of the LORD was kindled against Israel, and He moved David against them to say, "Go, number Israel and Judah."* If the theologians did gymnastics over Isaiah 45, you should see what they do over this. The plain reading is that Yahweh (LORD) was angry with Israel and incited David to sin by numbering Israel's fighting men, so He could punish Israel. Some theologians go so far as to say that the real meaning is that God was angry because David numbered Israel, and an adversary from another country moved David to sin.

What is the problem with this passage? James 1:13, 14 say, *"Let no man say when he is tempted, 'I am tempted of God:' for God cannot be tempted with evil, neither tempts He any man: But every man is tempted, when he is drawn away of his own lust, and enticed."* As I understand it, the Greek says that God <u>Himself</u> never tempts any man. We find the key to the puzzle in the parallel passage in 1Chronicles 21:1 *And Satan stood up against Israel, and provoked David to number Israel.* It is quite apparent that God was angry with Israel and used Satan to incite David to number the fighting men of Israel. Both passages are true. God incited David through Satan to sin but He Himself never tempted anyone.

Did God have a good reason? Yes, and more than one good reason. I don't think He has ever done anything for just one reason, because He knows all the ramifications of every act all down through history and eternity. When David repented, God used the place that the avenging angel stopped as the place His temple would be built.

Was it God's plan for David to sin? Yes. Did David get disciplined? Yes. It was through David's pride that He fell to temptation, and God judged Him; so the fact that our sin is in God's plan in no way takes away our responsibility, or makes God evil.

In Romans chapter nine, Paul has a discussion on this very issue. He says that salvation is not of man who wills or works, but of God who shows mercy. He goes on to say that God shows mercy to whom He wants to show mercy, and He hardens those He wants to harden. Then he says in verse 19 *"You will say then to me, 'Why does He still find fault, for who has resisted His will?'"* I am told that in the Greek "Who has resisted His will" is a rhetorical question to which the answer is: no one has ever resisted God's will. So the question Paul asks is: "Why does God still find fault with man since what man has done is God's will."

Now obviously, we are not saying that man follows God's revealed will, but that is not His only will. Many Christians say God has a revealed will, a perfect will, and a permissive will. I do not see any evidence in scripture for a permissive will, but I see plenty of evidence against it. For a god to have a permissive will, he would have to be a smaller god who does not "know the end from the beginning." I believe only in the revealed will and the perfect will of God, because those are demonstrated in scripture and fit with an infinite God.

The revealed will of God is the scripture and what the Holy Spirit reveals to us, which will <u>always</u> line up with the Bible. I have heard some pastors say that God's revealed will is only the scripture and that God doesn't talk to us except through His Word, but God gave us the Holy Spirit for a purpose and He is not mute. There is little purpose in the

> There is little purpose in the Holy Spirit living in and filling us unless He can speak to us.

Holy Spirit living in and filling us unless He can speak to us. I have never heard the audible voice of God, but I hear Him often in my spirit correcting, teaching, and encouraging me.

The perfect will of God, on the other hand, is exactly what happens, exactly the way He planned it for His purposes, His glory, and His pleasure.

That means that the passage above is saying that since everyone is following God's perfect will, why does God still judge and punish. What reply does Paul give? *"No, but you little man, who are you that replies against God? Shall the thing formed say to Him that formed it, 'Why have You made me like this?' Does not the potter have power over the clay, of the same lump to make one vessel unto honor, and another unto dishonor?"* Paul is saying that when we ask this question we are being impertinent. We have no right to ask it because we are just clay and God is God.

We Americans seem to have a lot more problems with that than people in other countries, especially people living in a dictatorship. We think that because we have a right to vote we should have a say in everything, but God is a Dictator. Daniel 4:35 *All the inhabitants of the earth are reputed as nothing: and He does according to His will in the army of heaven, and among the inhabitants of the earth: and none can stay His hand, or say to Him, What are You doing?* That sounds like a dictator to me, and Peter confirms this in Acts 4:24 when He prays for boldness after being beaten. He doesn't use the usual word translated Lord, but uses *despotes,* which we would translate despot. He is reminding himself and the other believers that God is completely in control, and I am so happy He is.

Here are two more verses from Proverbs that show God's control over man:

Proverbs 16:9 *A man's heart devises his way: but the LORD directs his steps.*

Proverbs 20:24 *Man's goings are of the LORD; how can a man then understand his own way?*

God says that He is in control of what we do, but we still bear the responsibility for our thoughts and actions.

There is another well-known incident in King David's life that demonstrates God's control and David's culpability. David's sin with Bathsheba is a true story just as it is written and, at the same time, it is a very interesting allegory. Now I know that many of you have been taught not to deal with allegory, but remember that Paul says in Galatians that Hagar and Sarah are an allegory showing the difference between grace and law. Joseph's story in Genesis is a beautiful picture of Jesus, which could be called an allegory, and I don't know of anyone who has a problem with that.

Now we do have to be careful with allegory. We should never get doctrine from allegory, but we can illustrate doctrine found elsewhere in scripture with allegory. I believe that there is no such thing as a coincidence and, if you bear with me a few more minutes I think you will see what I mean.

Let me refresh your memory about what happened in this story. King David, a man after God's own heart, gets a little too proud and a little too lazy and stays home while his men go off to war. He is not in the battle. He is relaxing on the roof of his palace when he sees a beautiful woman bathing. He sends for her after finding out she is married. He already has five wives and a number of concubines, but wants to have her for a fling. I don't think he has any intention of marrying her at this point; he just wants the excitement of sex with a different beautiful woman.

It is my opinion that she wanted David also; I think you may see why when we meet her husband, who is a little less than romantic. She returns home after their liaison, and some weeks later sends a message to David that she is pregnant. David still has no intention of marrying her, so he sends for her husband, Uriah. He comes to David, who as a pretense questions him about the battle and then sends him home to have relations with his wife. They had no DNA testing back then, and Uriah would naturally think this child was his own if he had been home around the right time to father this child.

The next morning David finds out that Uriah spent the night at the palace door. David, in his backslidden condition, cannot understand this kind of commitment. David was a great fighter, but partly, like in the movies, to get the girl. He keeps Uriah there another day, which probably frustrated Uriah (think Rambo), and gets him drunk that night. David sends him home again thinking that this time he has finally fixed the problem.

The next morning he finds out he is foiled again. See what I mean about Bathsheba wanting David? After being gone at least a month, Uriah comes home to Jerusalem and doesn't even take time to say 'hi' to his wife. What a romantic! But Uriah drunk has more integrity than David does sober. David decides to end his problem and add to his harem at the same time. He sends Uriah back to Commander Joab with his own death warrant. Joab, following David's orders, puts Uriah in the hottest part of the battle where he is killed.

As soon as the mourning period is over, David marries Bathsheba but the whole sordid affair displeased the Lord, Who then sends Nathan the prophet to rebuke David. Nathan tells David the story of a poor man who has only one lamb, but lives in the same city as a rich man who has hundreds of sheep. A traveler visits the rich man, but the rich man doesn't want to waste one of his lambs, so he takes the poor man's only lamb to make a meal for the traveler.

David is incensed with this kind of callousness and says, "This man deserves to die!"

Nathan says, "You are the man," knowing full well that if David reacts badly, Nathan could lose his head.

David, because he truly is a man after God's own heart, says, "I have sinned." He makes no excuses as did his predecessor, Saul. He finds real repentance but God judges him for the rest of his natural life. He never again has the complete blessing of God. Amnon, one of his sons, rapes his daughter Tamar, Amnon's half sister. David does nothing because he really doesn't understand his forgiveness, so Tamar's full brother, Absalom, kills Amnon. David banishes Absalom, but eventually brings him back without allowing him into his presence. Absalom is angry and attempts a coup. Absalom is killed and David is devastated. Did God hold David accountable? Yes. Did God plan David's sin? Let's take a look.

Remember that there are no coincidences, and that God is in control of every detail. Names are very important in the Bible. David means "beloved". Jesse, his father means "rich". In the allegory, Jesse is the Father who owns all. David is the beloved son, Jesus. Now I know some of you are a bit uneasy at this point, but see this through. David sees Bathsheba, a beautiful woman, and wants her. Bathsheba means "daughter of the oath". She is the promised bride of Christ, the Church, and Jesus loves her as only God can, and wants her for His own.

What is Bathsheba doing? She is bathing. She is trying to get clean and impress David with her beauty. We are always trying to be good enough for God, or impress Him with our talents. Both are absurd as we cannot ever measure up to the righteousness of God, and all of our talents were given to us by God. Jesus loves her because of who He is, not because she impresses Him. David commits sin with Bathsheba. Jesus <u>never</u> committed sin, but He became sin for us. 2 Corinthians 5:21 *For He (The Father)has made Him (Jesus) to be sin for us, Who knew no sin; that we might be made the righteousness of God in Him.*

David had a problem: Bathsheba was married to Uriah and David could not marry her until Uriah was dead. Uriah means "flame of Yahweh". He represents the law, the perfect, unbending law of God. Uriah must die, and the law must die if the Church is to marry Christ. Colossians 2:14 *Blotting out the handwriting of ordinances that was against us, which was contrary to us, and took it out of the way, nailing it to His cross.* Once the law was out of the way, the Church was free to be engaged to Jesus Christ, and will one day be married to Him at the Marriage Supper of the Lamb.

Now seeing how perfectly this fits in each aspect, can you honestly look me in the eye and tell me that God did not design this, with all the meanings of the names and the way it plays out? Yet God holds David accountable and judges him. While David is forgiven, the consequences play out for the rest of his life.

So what does all this have to do with having the peace of God? Let's go back to Romans 8:28 *And we know that all things work together for good to them that love God, to them who are the called according to His purpose.* "All things" means everything of which God is in control, and I think we have established that nothing has ever happened outside of His control. That means that the evil things that happen to us are under His control and that they are a part of His plan.

All things work together for <u>good</u>. What is the highest good for a human being? Our highest good is to glorify and magnify the Lord. What exactly does that mean? To glorify means to bring glory. Glory is praise and honor. We are not talking of the "Glory of God" which is intrinsic and indefinable, but the glory which we can give God. Our highest good is to bring glory to and magnify our God. When I ask people what it means to magnify they usually reply, "to make bigger", but that is incorrect. If I use a magnifying glass, microscope or telescope, I am magnifying an object. I do not change the size of the object, but I cause it to be seen more clearly and closely. We cannot change the size of our infinite God, and we don't want to when we see how great He really is; but when people see our God more clearly and closely, some of them want Him. They are the elect. Some run away and some scoff. Some of them may be elect for a later date, while others are not.

If glorifying and magnifying our God is the highest and greatest good, then any situation where it is possible for me to do that; works for good. Notice that it says good– not comfort or enjoyment. I remember a lady in our church asking one of our pastors, "Did God plan for me to be raped?"

He gently replied "Yes."

Her reply was, "Thank you."

> "Did God plan for me to be raped?"

Why? Because she understood that if it was not God's plan, then He either did not care enough, was not strong enough, or was not wise enough to stop it, and she wanted a God whom she could trust. She wanted a God who lovingly planned and went with her through the horror of rape for the good that He would bring out of it. She now works with other rape victims to help them heal through God's amazing love.

Understand that God never forces anyone to sin, but He uses their sinful desires to do things that will in the end turn out for His glory and He holds them responsible for their sin. Sin violates God's revealed will, but is part of His perfect will. Psalm 76:10 *Surely the wrath of man shall praise You: the remainder of wrath shall You restrain.* God uses man's sin that fits His plan and restrains the rest.

God plans for bad things to happen so He can show His glory and power. We don't always see the good, in this life, and it doesn't often happen as quickly as it does in this next story, but God promises it will come. When Jesus was told that His friend, Lazarus, was very ill; He purposely waited two more days before going to Bethany, where Lazarus lived. He did this so that Lazarus would die and remain dead four days before He raised him back to life, giving glory to God. This was very hard on Lazarus and his two sisters, Mary and Martha, but Jesus went to them, and wept with them, and comforted them, before raising Lazarus back to life. He puts us through great trials for His good purpose, but He goes through the trials with us and holds us close if we are willing.

I have heard hundreds of Christians, including many pastors, say that God underlines bad things to happen but He does not plan them. I heard one famous radio pastor say that not a blade of grass moves on the planet without God's control–and then he turned right around and said God allows bad things in our lives. Why would a loving, all-knowing, all-powerful God allow something in our lives that He did not plan?

I realize that it is politically correct among believers to use this word "allow", but that does not make it right. For God to allow something in our lives that He did not plan or want, someone else would have to come up with the idea and then sell God on the idea.

Usually Satan is credited with coming up with the idea, and then somehow talks God into it. That is blasphemy and heresy! Our God cannot learn anything because He already knows everything. Jesus as a man learned, but as God, He always knew everything that would ever happen. God is the only person in the universe that ever had an original thought, so how can anyone else come up with something for God to allow?

I have heard people point to Job as proof that Satan comes up with plans that God allows. Let's take a look at what it really says.

Job 1:6 *Now there was a day when the sons of God came to present themselves before the LORD, and Satan came also among them.*

The angels came to report to God, and Satan came with them. Some people think Satan doesn't have access to God, but how else would he be "the accuser of the brethren?"

Job 1:7, 8 *And the LORD said unto Satan, "From where do you come?" Then Satan answered the LORD, and said, "From going to and fro in the earth, and from walking up and down in it." And the LORD said unto Satan, "Have you considered My servant Job, that there is none like him in the earth, a perfect and an upright man, one that fears God, and avoids evil?"*

Who posed the question? Did Satan ask God about Job? No! God asked the questions, and God has <u>never</u> asked a question to which He did not know the answer. God asked Satan about Job because God had a plan that He wanted to use Satan to implement.

Job 1:9-11 *Then Satan answered the LORD, and said, "Does Job fear God for nothing? Have You not made a hedge about him, and about his house, and about all that he has on every side? You have blessed the work of his hands, and his substance is increased in the land. But put forth Your hand now, and touch all that he has, and he will curse You to Your face."*

Satan tells God that if God will take away all that Job has, Job will curse Him.

Job 1:12 *And the LORD said unto Satan, Behold, all that he has is in your power; only upon himself put not forth your hand. So Satan left the presence of the LORD.*

God puts it right back in Satan's lap, but puts specific limits on what Satan can do. Did Satan get God to do something that God did not want to do? No way! God used Satan to accomplish something that He wanted to do in Job's life so that Job would say, "*I had heard of You by the hearing of the ear: but now my eye sees You. Wherefore I abhor myself, and repent in dust and ashes."* Job 42:5, 6. Satan is God's unwilling servant whom God uses for His own glory.

God's plan, God's way, in God's timing is always the way things go. How else could God say, "*My brethren, count it all joy when you fall into various temptations,"* James 1:2. He is in full control of every temptation and tribulation and sends them for His purposes. *And not only so, but we glory in tribulations also: knowing that tribulation works patience; and patience, experience; and experience, hope: and hope makes us unashamed; because the love of God is shed abroad in our hearts by the Holy Spirit which is given unto us.* Romans 5:3-5

My sister, Becky Santa, a year and nine months older than I am, went to be with Jesus on the 17th of January of 2010, two weeks after her fifty-ninth birthday. We were very close growing up, and continued a great relationship though she lived in Southern California and I live in Oregon. The last name Santa saved her from a ticket one Christmas Eve. She was in too big a hurry and got pulled over. When the policeman saw the name on her license, he laughed and handed it back and said, "I can't give a ticket to Mrs. Santa on Christmas Eve."

'How are we going to use this cancer to serve the Lord?"

In May of 2006 when she was diagnosed with cancer and given less than six months to live, she turned to her husband, Bob and said, "How are we going to use this to serve the Lord?" She kept that attitude through 4 years of radiation and chemotherapy. She wrote a paper on *"The Privilege of Having Cancer."* In it she wrote about being able to talk about Jesus to other cancer patients who wouldn't listen to anyone who didn't have cancer.

She was a great baker and loved to bake cookies. She turned that into a ministry where she would take cookies to people fighting cancer so she could share Jesus with them. She found a paper on the internet written by John Piper called *"Don't Waste Your Cancer".* It is a great paper on the sovereignty of God and how he gives cancer (or any other problem for that matter) for His good purpose. I have handed out many of those papers to people with varying problems.

Becky and I both love hymns, and she especially loved hymns about Heaven during those years. When her time drew close, all of the family that could, gathered around her. She was well loved. On the eve of January 16, the whole family was singing hymns. As it got late and she was still hanging on, but sleeping, everyone went to bed.

We have twin sisters: Debbie and Ruth who both graduated from Biola's Nursing Program and are wonderful nurses today. They were sleeping on either side of her when early in the morning she gave a slight cough. Ruth came to her and heard her peacefully breathe out her last breath. "Oh Becky, you went home," Ruth whispered.

Of course we miss her, but we know she is with her Redeemer and Friend, Jesus Christ. So we don't feel sorry for her, but we are a little jealous. We know that God will take us home in His timing, and we need to enjoy the life and fellowship with Him and with each other until that time.

So how can we have the peace of God in every situation? First, we need to know that this situation comes through the mighty and loving hand of our Father for His good purpose. We don't need to understand the purpose, though we should look for it in ways that we can glorify Him through the situation.

Second, we need to see if His purpose is disciplinary. Is there something we are doing that is wrong, or something we are not doing that we should be doing?

Third, we need to thank Him for the situation.

"What? Are you crazy?" No, this is one of the evidences of being filled with the Spirit in Ephesians 5:20 *Giving thanks <u>always for all things</u> unto God and the Father in the name of our Lord Jesus Christ.* "But I can't!" Yes, you can, with His strength, by being filled with His Spirit.

Philippians 4:13 *I can do all things through Christ who strengthens me.* Paul's context here is attitude. He is not saying we can win the Olympics or make a million dollars. Look at the context–it's all about

> No matter what the circumstances are, I can have the right attitude.

attitude. When he says, "I can do anything," he is saying that no matter what the circumstances are, I can have the right attitude, which will glorify the Father and His Son, Jesus Christ–but only through His strength. I may be able to do it for a short time on my own, but I can keep going in His strength forever because His strength is limitless.

Fourth, I need to pray about how to use this circumstance to serve God and others. Often it is through our healing and then helping others who have a similar problem to heal.

My addiction to pornography was my fault. I can come up with reasons why I was curious, and people and circumstances who contributed to it, but the bottom line is that I knew it was wrong and I did it anyway. It affected my walk with Christ, my ministry, my marriage and my family. Was it part of God's plan? Yes, and He is using me with many men, and some women, who have sexual addictions. I counsel in our church, I started an ongoing group called *"Fully Alive"* that helps men get out of sexual addiction, and I work with "Celebrate Recovery" to help people get free in Jesus from all kinds of "hurts, habits, and hang-ups".

This summer (2011) I will return to Iquitos, Peru, God willing, to help introduce "Celebrate Recovery" there. God is using what He planned before the world began, to accomplish other things that He planned before the world began. Ephesians 2:10 *For we are His workmanship, created in Christ Jesus for good works, which God has before ordained that we should walk in them.*

I am nobody special, and I think that is why God uses me. That way He gets the glory. Romans 7:18 *For I know that in me (that is, in my flesh,) dwells no good thing.* In my flesh, my old nature, I am a scumball and you wouldn't want to know me. If not for the grace of God, I would be dead or in prison. I know my own depravity because of my thought life and I am grateful because I grew up thinking that I was pretty good. I don't have that illusion any more so it is easy for me to forgive. I know that I have sinned a whole lot more against God than anyone can sin against me; and He has completely forgiven me.

A song came out a few years back by Ray Boltz entitled *"One Drop of Blood."* I understand his premise that Jesus' blood is powerful, but the song is not biblical. It took the death of Jesus just to save me. Not one person could have been saved without the death of Jesus. Jesus could not have pricked His finger and saved anyone. He had to die. Ray may have thought that he was good enough that Jesus didn't have to do much to save him, I don't know, but he gave himself some kind of excuse to go into homosexuality. I hope and pray he repents and returns to God. I love most of the songs he wrote and sang, but he is certainly not living for Jesus now.

> Not one person could have been saved without the death of Jesus.

Is Ray still going to Heaven? If he was a Christian, and I have a hard time thinking that a non-believer could write some of those songs, then he is still on his way. Because we don't save ourselves, and only God can–it is forever.

What is his problem? He doesn't know the purpose of life. He apparently thinks that pleasure trumps all. He claims that God made him gay. Most Christians would argue against that, saying that no one is born gay. The scripture says that we are all born sinners. I was born with a desire to take what is yours and get my pleasure at your expense. If I don't fight my desires with God's power, I will carry them out and hurt you. The only way I can successfully fight my desires is through surrendering on a daily, hourly and many times a minute-by-minute basis. Through the Spirit, by the power of the death and resurrection of Jesus, I need to keep surrendering to God and resisting the devil–and so does anyone who is tempted by homosexuality or any other sin.

Many Christians believe that homosexuality is a worse sin than any other because God calls it an abomination. But let's take a look at what else God calls an abomination: eating lobster, offering an animal with any blemish, wearing the clothing of the opposite sex, having dishonest weights or measures, doing unrighteous acts and being unyielding to authority.

I think that puts a little different idea on what God calls an abomination. In other words, as far as God is concerned, if we habitually are unyielding to authority by speeding when we drive, we are as much an abomination as a homosexual. God looks at all sin as equally bad. Lust, laziness, and gluttony, some sins I deal with on a regular basis, are as bad as homosexuality.

The only way God differentiates between sins to my knowledge is on the basis of the knowledge of the individual. In Luke 12:43-48, Jesus tells a story of servants who disobey their master's will. The one who knew his master's will was beaten with many stripes, while the one who did not know his master's will was beaten with few stripes. We as believers will never be punished for our sin, but in this life we will be disciplined by the loving hand of our Father. There are times that it feels more like punishment because it really hurts, but it is only from God's love that He disciplines us.

The only way we as believers can properly differentiate between sins is by results. An example is: if I think about committing adultery, God says it is just as bad as doing it; however, it doesn't affect nearly as many people as if I carry it

> I have been disciplined many times for enjoying my temptations.

out. All sin starts with thoughts, so we need to take every thought captive to Jesus. I have been disciplined many times for enjoying my temptations. I thank God that through His grace I have not acted them out. I realize that if I did, I would ruin my marriage, my family, my ministry, and my career, for a few minutes of pleasure.

Notice King David's progression in Psalm 51, which is the song he wrote after confessing his sin with Bathsheba.

Psalm 51:1, 2 *Have mercy upon me, O God, according to Your loving-kindness: according unto the multitude of Your tender mercies blot out my transgressions. Wash me thoroughly from my iniquity, and cleanse me from my sin.*

He wants washing and cleansing which only God can give. He wants to feel clean again.

Psalm 51:10 *Create in me a clean heart, O God; and renew a right spirit within me.*

Here David is asking not to be cleaned but to have a clean heart, a righteous spirit; in other words, a new nature. He wants to be good from the inside out.

Psalm 51:13 *Then will I teach transgressors Your ways; and sinners shall be converted unto You.*

Now David wants to be used to help others find their way to God. This is what each of us need: to know our forgiveness, to understand who we are in Christ so we live as a new creation instead of just "sinners saved by grace", and to be used by our Creator to tell others about Him.

When we understand who we are and how much God loves us, all of our fears disappear and we relax in the loving arms of our Father. At the same time, we are empowered by His Spirit to be used to share Him with others.

Chapter Four

Faith That Prays

Why pray?

If God is in control of every situation and knows everything that will happen, why should I pray? Most people misunderstand the purpose of prayer. They take verses like James 5:16-18 *Confess your faults one to another, and pray one for another, that you may be healed. The effectual fervent prayer of a righteous man avails much. Elijah was a man subject to like passions as we are, and he prayed earnestly that it might not rain: and it rained not on the earth by the space of three years and six months .And he prayed again, and the heaven gave rain, and the earth brought forth her fruit.* They use verses like this to say that Elijah got God to do something other than what God had planned, but that is because they don't really read the scriptures. 1Kings 18:36 says, *"And it came to pass at the time of the offering of the evening sacrifice, that Elijah the prophet came near, and said, 'LORD God of Abraham, Isaac, and of Israel, let it be known this day that You are God in Israel, and that I am Your servant, and that I have done all these things <u>at Your word.</u>'"* That means that God told Elijah what to do and Elijah did it, bringing Israel back to the Lord. Was Elijah's prayer effective? Yes, but it was effective because it was according to God's will. 1 John 5:14 *And* *this is the confidence that we have in Him, that, if we ask any thing __according to His will__, He hears us.* We do not pray to change God's mind. We pray to increase our intimacy with God so that we know His will better.

A well-known evangelist came to our church one time and received word that a friend of his had a brain tumor. He gathered a number of us around to pray for his friend, and then he said something very strange. "I don't want to hear anyone pray 'If it's Your will.'" I prayed silently so as not to offend and I think I understand his thinking, but he was wrong. Like many Christians, I think he was afraid of giving God an out. That is how some view using the words "if it is Your will".

There are two main scriptures on this subject. The first is Luke 22:42 where Jesus is praying in the garden *Saying, "Father, if You are willing, remove this cup from Me, nevertheless not My will, but Yours, be done."* Here Jesus, God in human flesh, is asking His Father to remove the awful cup of suffering He is about to go through, but notice He says "If You are willing," and, "Not My will but Yours be done."

> We have no leg to stand on when we want our way instead of God's way.

If Jesus could say that, at His hour of deepest need, certainly we should be able to say it. He never deserved anything but glory, while we, in ourselves, deserve only Hell. We have no leg to stand on when we want our way instead of God's way, whether we are praying for ourselves or others.

The second passage is in James 4:13-17 *Come now, you that say, Today or tomorrow we will go into such a city, and continue there a year, and buy and sell, and get gain: for you know not what shall be tomorrow. For what is your life? It is even a vapor, which appears for a little time, and then vanishes away. For you ought to say, If the Lord wills, we shall live, and do this, or that. But now you rejoice in your boastings: all such rejoicing is evil. Therefore to him that knows to do good, and does not do it, to him it is sin.*

Now while this is not specifically talking about prayer, it obviously applies. If when we are talking with each other we need to say, "If God wills," how much more should we say it when talking to the King Himself. And notice the last verse. If we know that we should do it and we don't, we are sinning.

I had a young Christian man in my office the other day who was adamant that if you just believed enough that you already have what you ask for, God has to give it to you. Is that really the kind of faith God is after? Or is He after the faith that says, "Father, I trust You to do what is best for me to be most able to glorify You?"

Currently I am praying about my wrist that was dislocated in the fall. (If that is news to you, you forgot to read the introduction.) As my hand bent back, the scaphoid and lunate bones moved forward and stayed forward as my hand went back to normal position. No one in Grants Pass had seen anything like it, and all of the surgeons in Medford except one turned me down. This surgeon wanted to remove those bones because she is fairly certain that they do not have blood supply, and therefore won't live. I opted to leave them in at this point and see if God wants to do a miracle and make them live. I am not sure that she is a believer, and this might be a way to bring her to Christ. But my prayer is for God to do what is best. He may want to give me a permanent reminder to keep my thoughts pure and on Him. He may want the surgeon to see that I still trust Him even if the bones have to be removed and the wrist has to be fused.

How to pray
It has been said that immature Christians spend most of their time in prayer on themselves, intermediate believers on others, and mature believers on adoration of God Himself. I agree.

There is nothing wrong with praying for ourselves. We need to confess our sin. We need to pray for wisdom, strength, patience, love, and whatever else with which we happen to be struggling. There is nothing wrong with asking for things with which we can glorify God as long

> Immature Christians spend most of their time in prayer on themselves, intermediate believers on others and mature believers on adoration of God Himself.

as we are open to whatever He wants. However, if that is the bulk of our prayer, we are still self-focused and need to grow up.

We need to pray for others. Samuel said, "*God forbid that I should sin against the LORD in ceasing to pray for*

you." You say, "Yeah, but he was a priest." So are you!
1Peter 2:9 *But you are a chosen generation, a royal
<u>priesthood</u>, an holy nation, a peculiar people; that you
should show forth the praises of Him Who has called you
out of darkness into His marvelous light!*

We all need prayer because that is how God's power is
unleashed. Again, it does not change His mind, but He
has chosen to use our prayer, in some spiritual way that I
don't understand, to accomplish His purposes. I need
people praying for me. You need people praying for you.
It is important for us to pray for others and the prayers in
Paul's epistles are a great way to start.

The most important thing we can do in prayer, however,
is to praise and adore Almighty God. When we adore
Him for Who He is, and praise Him for what He has
done, we find that we are fulfilled and we fit well as His
children. I love to sing praise hymns and choruses to Him
as I kneel before Him. If you can't kneel, God
understands. You can pray in any position you want. I
know several prayer warriors who walk while they pray.
It helps keep them awake.

I like the acronym ACTS. It stands for **A**doration,
Confession, **T**hanksgiving and **S**upplication. Those are
the essential parts of prayer. We don't always have to do
them in order. A lot of times I put confession first so my
mind and heart are more ready to praise Him, but CATS
doesn't sound as spiritual as ACTS.

Adoration

Adoration is concentrating on the character of God and enjoying being with Him because of <u>Who He is</u>. He told Moses, "I am that I am," meaning that He is the self-existent One, but it also includes all of the "I am's" in scripture; like when Jesus said I am the Way, the Truth, and the Life, I am the Door, I am the Good Shepherd, I am the Light of the world, I am the Bread of life, I am the true Vine, and I am the Son of God. Every name of God you find in scripture is included. We would do well to find them, make a list of them, and take one or two of them each day and meditate on them in adoration of who God really is, so that we are not worshipping a god that we made up, but the true God of the Bible.

If you know the hymns, sing them to God. If you don't know them, I suggest that you beg, borrow or buy a good hymnal and read a hymn of worship each day as you start your prayer time. You don't have to use hymns, but they do help me. You don't have to be old to enjoy the adoration and majesty of the hymns.

There are also many modern choruses that will help you prepare your heart for worship and the Psalms of adoration are a wonderful way to get your heart right for worshipping our Father. Paul mentions psalms, hymns, and spiritual songs in Ephesians; all of which are useful and speaking or singing them is a supernatural result of being filled with the Holy Spirit.

Confession

We talked about confession in chapter two, *"Faith that Triumphs"* so I will be brief here. Of course we need to be agreeing with God about the sin of which we are already aware, and asking for His strength to triumph, but we also need to be looking into our lives to see if there are things we have not yet seen that He will convict us about if we are willing. It is a lot like marriage. If I don't ask my wife how I'm doing from time to time, I won't know on what I should be working to change.

We also need to be asking God to search us as the psalmist wrote, *"Search me, O God, and know my heart: try me, and know my thoughts: And see if there is any wicked way in me, and lead me in the way everlasting."* Psalm 139:23, 24. If we really love God and truly want to please Him, we should be asking Him to help us see what we need Him to change in our lives.

Thanksgiving

Thankfulness is the key to joy. We will never have real joy, the deep joy that sustains us through every trial, temptation, and sorrow, unless we are truly thankful. I'm not just referring to

> Thankfulness is the key to joy.

being thankful for the things for which we think we should be thankful, but for everything that comes into our lives. That is what God requires.

2 Corinthians 2:14 *Now thanks be unto God, Who always causes us to triumph in Christ, and makes manifest the fragrance of His knowledge by us in every place.*

Thank God for the victory we find in the knowledge of Him. Notice the sweet fragrance of knowing Him and how it enhances our lives.

2 Corinthians 9:15 *Thanks be unto God for His indescribable gift.*

We can never thank God enough for sending His Son, the Creator of all things, to die in our place and give us eternal life and all the blessings and inheritance we have in Him.

Ephesians 5:20 *Giving thanks always for all things unto God and the Father in the name of our Lord Jesus Christ.*

God did not misspeak here; He actually wants us to give thanks for trials, tribulations, sorrows, and horrible things as well as the pleasant things. When we realize that this life is just preparation for the next, and we are only strangers and pilgrims here, and all of the things we encounter are from the loving hand of our Father, we can give thanks for everything and, in doing that, we will find true joy.

Philippians 4:6 *Be anxious for nothing; but in every thing by prayer and supplication with thanksgiving let your requests be made known unto God.*

Be anxious for how much? Nothing! Is that possible? If you are used to worrying about everything this seems impossible, but if we learn who God really is and learn to trust Him, we can learn to stop worrying. The attitude of thanksgiving always needs to go along with our supplication.

Colossians 2:7 *Rooted and built up in Him, and established in the faith, as you have been taught, abounding therein with thanksgiving.*

If we are rooted in Jesus the true vine and built on the foundation of Jesus, we will abound with thanksgiving.

Colossians 3:17 *And whatsoever you do in word or deed, do all in the name of the Lord Jesus, giving thanks to God and the Father by Him.*

In everything we do, we should be thankful that God has gifted us to be able to do those things. I have a friend named Skip who has multiple sclerosis and has been in a wheelchair for many years, but every time I see him he is so grateful for what he can do. He is in a facility about thirty-five miles from my house, so I don't see him often enough, but every time I do I come away more encouraged than he does, I'm sure. He uses every chance he gets to tell people of Jesus' love. His gratefulness is an example to me.

1 Thessalonians 3:9 *For what thanks can we give to God again for you, for all the joy with which we joy for your sakes before our God.*

The joy we have from the fellowship of other believers and the intimacy we can have with those who care enough to hold us accountable, are truly amazing and worth endless gratitude.

1Thessalonians 5:18 *In everything give thanks: for this is the will of God in Christ Jesus concerning you.*

This is the counterpart to "give thanks for everything" and is used by many without regard for Ephesians 5:20 to say that we have to be thankful only in situations and not for situations. However, when we learn to be grateful for the sorrows and pain, we find true freedom and joy.

1 Timothy 4:4, 5 *For every creature of God is good, and nothing is to be refused, if it is received with thanksgiving: for it is sanctified by the word of God and prayer.*

This is one of the main passages showing that we should give thanks before eating. I love to see families in restaurants bow their heads and pray before eating, and I will usually tell them so. I remember there were two extremes to fall into at lunch when I was in school. One was to pretend to tie one's shoe while praying, and the other was to bow one's head and count to ten. We should be so grateful for what God has given us, and so proud of our Father that we are not ashamed to be seen praying, and we should have plenty for which to thank Him as well.

Hebrews 13:15 *By Him therefore let us offer the sacrifice of praise to God continually, that is, the fruit of our lips giving thanks to His name.*

Continual praise and thanks should be quite natural, but often it is so easy to join in with others who are complaining and grumbling. In such situations, we should be the ones to bring the subject back to gratefulness. That is one way we can offer the sacrifice of praise. It's not easy to do, and that is what makes it a sacrifice.

Supplication

Habakkuk 2:20 *But the LORD is in His holy temple: let all the earth keep silence before Him.* Before we start asking God for the things and situations about which we are concerned, we should spend some time in silence listening to what the Holy Spirit has to say. Remember that we need to pray

> Before we start asking God, we should spend some time in silence listening to the Holy Spirit.

according to God's will, and the Spirit, as God, can inform us what His will is on the matters at hand and bring to mind matters of which we are not yet thinking. Spending time in silence before our Father is an excellent way to prepare for the day. Too often we tell God our plans and ask Him to bless them instead of asking Him what His plans are for us. We will have much more success if we find and follow His plans.

After the silence, we can begin asking God for the things we feel are His will and we should not be afraid to ask great and grand things if they are truly for His glory. After all, He is our Father and Paul said, *"Charge them that are rich in this world, that they be not high minded, nor trust in uncertain riches, but in the living God, who gives us richly all things to enjoy."* 1 Timothy 6:17

God does enjoy giving gifts to His children. Again Paul says in Romans 8:32 *"He that spared not His own Son, but delivered Him up for us all, how shall He not along with Him also freely give us all things?"* We just need to be careful that we are truly seeking His will and not our own. We also need to hold things with an open hand so it doesn't hurt when God takes it away. Another consideration when God gives us something is this: does God intend us to keep it or are we to bless someone else with it?

It is a great idea to keep a prayer journal so that we can look back and see what God has done. Many times in the Psalms David is feeling depressed or afraid and he reminds himself of God's past deliverance and comes out with greater faith knowing that God will deliver him again.

Always remember that proper prayer will help us to draw near to our Father and change us to be more like Jesus by being filled with the Holy Spirit. Prayer should not be limited to a special time of day, as important as that is; it should be constant all day long, in every decision, in every trial, in every joy, and in every sorrow. Prayer is the key to faith and to change in our lives.

Chapter Five

Faith That Works

So if we don't have to be good to be saved, and nothing we do can please God before we are saved, where do works fit in? Remember that we were dead before God made us alive. We had an old nature (called our flesh in scripture) that was very much alive, and even when we were doing things that the world calls good, we did them for the wrong reasons: to feel better about ourselves or to be seen as good by God or by people. Whatever our reason may be, God called all of our works filthy rags. Isaiah 64:6 *But we are all as an unclean thing, and all our righteousnesses are as filthy rags; and we all do fade as a leaf; and our iniquities, like the wind, have taken us away.* The Hebrew words for filthy rags actually mean menstrual cloths. That is how much God hates our own righteousness. He doesn't even want to see it.

However, now that we have been saved, our old nature was nailed to the cross and it is dead as we talked about in chapter two, *"Faith that Triumphs"*. We are alive in Christ with our new nature which I believe is our spirit. John 3:6 *That which is born of the flesh is flesh; and that which is born of the Spirit is spirit.* In other words, when we are born physically, we have a body and a soul. When we are "born again" our spirit is born from above. We are

103

now related to God, we are His children, born and adopted into His family. We have the nature though not the power, of God. Don't misunderstand, we will never be God but we have His nature in us. One illustration is electricity. I can have a million volts going through my body without harm as long as the amperage is low enough. Raise the amperage and I'll be dead. We have the voltage but not the amperage of God.

Even with our new nature we still need to be filled with His Spirit. Galatians 3:2, 3 *This only would I learn of you, Did you receive the Spirit by the works of the law, or by the hearing of faith? Are you so foolish? Having begun in the Spirit, are you now made perfect by the flesh?* We so easily go back to the old thinking that we need to do things to mature in the Christian life or to please God. It is always our faith that pleases God. Our works must come from our faith with the power and filling of the Spirit.

 We need the fruit of the Spirit in our lives for any of our works to be of worth, and we can only have that fruit with the filling of the Spirit. Galatians 5:22, 23 *But the fruit of the Spirit is love, joy, peace, longsuffering, gentleness, goodness, faith, meekness, temperance: against such there is no law.*

Our new nature, our spirit, can do no wrong; it is the very righteousness of Christ. 2 Corinthians 5:21 *For He has made Him to be sin for us, Who knew no sin; that we become the righteousness of God in Him.* It is in this righteousness that we now can do works that please God–works for which we will be rewarded.

What a marvelous God we have! He chooses us, who are mired in sin, not based on who we are but on Who He is, forgives all our sin, brings us into His family, gives us a nature that can do only good works, and then rewards us for the things we do for and through Him!

Now, I've heard some Christians say, "I don't want any rewards, it's enough to be with Jesus." They don't understand what the rewards are about. I once heard a radio preacher put it this way: he had been stationed in Germany while he was in the army and had a commander who was also a believer. His commander was always after him to work for ribbons and medals, many of which he really did not care about; but he worked hard for them because they reflected well on his commander.

In the same way, the rewards we will receive will bring glory to our Commander-in-Chief, our Lord and Savior, Jesus Christ. He took a scumball like me and turned me into a servant and friend, by His grace worthy to reign with Him. He gets all of the glory and I get none, and that is just the way it should be. Do I still have to deal with my old nature? Yes, and I will until I go to be with Him. I am grateful to God that most of my sins are only sins of the mind and don't become actions or words as much as in my past, but they are still sin and I must continue to battle, but I win only with His power.

In Matthew 5:16 Jesus said, *"Let your light so shine before men, that they may see your good works, and glorify your Father Who is in heaven."* When we do good works, our light shines because we are reflecting the

Light of the world, Jesus. We are like the moon reflecting the sun. We have no light in ourselves, but Jesus shines through us as we deal with the sin in our lives and we cultivate the fruit of the Spirit. This causes people to glorify God and allows us to be part of His plan to save them.

Philippians 2:12 *Wherefore, my beloved, as you have always obeyed, not as in my presence only, but now much more in my absence, work out your own salvation with fear and trembling.* What does this mean? Notice that it does not say "work for" but "work out" your salvation. The idea here is that after we have been saved, we have God's salvation, but it needs to be worked out into our lives so that people can see it.

James 2:24 *You see then how that by works a man is justified, and not by faith only.* Now here in James we have an apparent problem. Are we justified by faith plus works? It is a big enough problem that Martin Luther did not consider James to be inspired. So how do we deal with this problem? What does James mean by justification? Is he talking about being justified before God?

Let's take a look at a few more verses in the same chapter. James 2:21-23 *Was not Abraham our father justified by works, when he had offered Isaac his son upon the altar? Do you see how faith combined with his works, and by works was faith made perfect? And the scripture was fulfilled which says, "Abraham believed God, and it was counted unto him for righteousness: and he was called the friend of God."*

It is important to notice there are about thirty years between the two things that James mentions. God counted Abraham's faith as righteousness before he had been in the Promised Land ten years in Genesis 15:6 *And he believed in the LORD; and He counted it to him for righteousness.* It was another fifteen years before Isaac was born, and Isaac was probably about fifteen when his father was told to sacrifice him.

So Abraham was counted righteous by God long before his work completed or "made perfect" his faith. Therefore we are not talking about justification by God. God didn't test Abraham to find out if he would obey; God knows the end from the beginning. He tested Abraham for a number of reasons: so Abraham would have to go through it and see how much he trusted God, so his faith would grow, so we could see Abraham's faith, see the picture of the father offering the son, and see the substitutionary death of the ram in place of the son.

So God is doing this for our benefit and that is the point in James. Our faith justifies us before God and our works justify us before men. Without works no one can tell whether or not we are believers. Matthew 7:20 *Wherefore by their fruits you shall know them.* Although this is actually a negative teaching about false teachers it still fits that we as believers are known by our works.

And this goes along with Proverbs 20:11 *Even a child is known by his doings, whether his work is pure, and whether it is right.* How we are seen by others reflects on our Father and gives us opportunities to speak for Him, but if we don't have the faith to speak for Him, we really need to grow our faith.

Chapter Six

Faith That Speaks

There are only two important things for us to do while we are still in this life–grow our faith and share our faith, neither of which is possible in Heaven. Everything we have been talking about falls into these two categories. In Heaven everyone will know Jesus, so there will be no need for us to share our faith in the same way we can now. Jeremiah 31:34 *"And they shall teach no more every man his neighbor, and every man his brother, saying, 'Know the LORD': for they shall all know Me, from the least of them unto the greatest of them," says the LORD.*

We will have no need to grow our faith in heaven because we will see Him face to Face, and our sin nature will be completely gone. 1Corinthians13:12 *For now we see through a glass, darkly; but then face to face: now I know in part; but then shall I know even as also I am known.*

> Anything that does not somehow relate to growing or sharing our faith is a waste of time, life, breath, and energy.

Anything in this life that does not somehow relate to growing or sharing our faith is a waste of time, life, breath, and energy. We are put here to learn to know and trust God more and to share Him with others. Now I am not saying that life has to become boring, or that we need to spend all of our time in ascetic practices. Quite the opposite! What I am saying is that God has gifted each of us differently, and has given us different interests for His purposes, not ours. Life becomes very exciting when we start using our gifts and talents for His purposes. Our job, our school, our hobbies, our sports and our homes, when given to Him for His glory, will fill and fulfill us beyond our wildest dreams, but if we use them to fulfill us, we will find that they never really satisfy. Matthew 6:33 *But seek first the kingdom of God, and His righteousness; and all these things shall be added unto you.*

Remember that God's ways are usually the opposite of our ways: "lose your life to find it," "the meek will inherit the earth," and "to be first become the servant of all." God's economy works perfectly, but does not fit with this world's wisdom. The world says: "you deserve a break today," "look out for number one," and "you're worth it." Follow the world's wisdom and you will always fall short of real satisfaction. Follow God's wisdom and you will have peace through heartache, joy through pain and real fulfillment. Sometimes it's like the achy, tired feeling of satisfaction after a day of accomplishing something important, compared to the wiped-out feeling of dissatisfaction after a day of trying to have fun by pleasing ourselves.

So what does this have to do with Faith that speaks? We have already talked about faith that works, and many times when we are doing the right things and having a good attitude, people may think we are a good, religious person, but not have a clue what we believe or Who really makes us tick. We need to speak the truth of God, as well as live it.

The high priest's robe in the Old Testament had alternating gold bells and pomegranates sewn into the hem showing that talking the walk (the bells) and walking the talk (the fruit) are equally important. So many people love to quote, "Preach the word always and if necessary use words" because they are afraid to speak up about Jesus. It is just as necessary to use words as to live right. Sure, sometimes people will ask us about the "reason for the hope we have," but that won't happen very often. We need to be praying for the opportunities.

"Wait a minute," you say, "What is the point of witnessing if God has predetermined who is going to heaven?" First and most important, obedience is the point. God doesn't need us to do anything, but He has planned to use us and he commanded us to make disciples. Matthew 28:19, 20 *Go therefore, and teach all nations, baptizing them in the name of the Father, and of the Son, and of the Holy Spirit: Teaching them to observe all things which I have commanded you: and, see, I am with you always, even unto the end of the world. Amen. "Teach all nations"* is better translated "make disciples."

Obedience is always first. Many missionaries have gone to foreign lands because of the need, and they can never meet the need, so they burn out. If they went based on obedience to God's call, there would be no burn out, regardless of the circumstances, because they would be doing God's work, God's way, with God's power; and His power never burns out.

The circumstances are not important because the God who controls them is the one who has called us. That, of course, does not mean that we shouldn't try to change the things we can change, which should be changed. Over and over God sends things our way that we should not accept but should change, like in the first part of Niebuhr's famous prayer: "God, grant me the serenity to accept the things I cannot change, the courage to change the things I can, and the wisdom to know the difference."

> Our amazing God created us in such a way that we get our greatest fulfillment from glorifying Him.

The second reason for sharing our faith is that it brings our King glory. He is glorified when His light shines through us. Matthew 5:16 *Let your light so shine before men, that they may see your good works, and glorify your Father which is in Heaven.* This is the reason we live; this is why we were created. We should want to glorify our King without any kickbacks, but our amazing God created us in such a way that we get our greatest fulfillment from glorifying Him.

The third reason to witness is that people need Jesus, and we need to tell others about Him, but if you don't put obedience and God's glory first, you will not have the stamina to keep going and you will start believing that it is your responsibility to save people. When we are obedient, we leave the results to God and we can have complete peace while continuing to grow in our faith that causes us to speak of Him to those He puts in our path.

The last reason to witness is that being used by the God who made the universe is the most exciting thing we can do, and the greatest privilege that is bestowed on humans. It is one of the two things that we can participate in, which have eternal ramifications. The other is making babies; because every baby made will exist for eternity, either in Heaven or Hell. Being able to be a partner with God in bringing a person to faith in Christ trumps everything else in life.

While writing this book, a good friend of mine called and recommended a book for me to read. It is called "*Love Wins,*" written by Rob Bell. We have watched many of Rob's thought-provoking videos at our church and I have had great respect for him. However, I did not get past the preface before I realized that Rob has fallen into the trap of trying to make Christianity more palatable to unbelievers. His premise is that God loves us so much that He couldn't possibly send anyone to Hell for eternity.

In the book, Rob claims that many more would be believers if only we got rid of the idea of eternal punishment. He doesn't seem to understand that, from man's view, people will not come to God in this life if they can do what they want here and have another chance to get to Heaven after they die—or as in Rob's book, many chances. Why should my old nature pay any attention to a God who can't bear to punish me?

In the preface on page vii Rob says, "Jesus' story has been hijacked by a number of other stories, stories Jesus isn't interested in telling, because they have nothing to do with what he came to do. The plot has been lost, and it's time to reclaim it." He defines these stories on the next page as being stories indicating that "a select few Christians will spend forever in a peaceful, joyous place called heaven, while the rest of humanity spends forever in torment and punishment in hell with no chance for anything better."

Jesus isn't interested in telling this story? It was one of His main themes! Jesus talked more about Hell than He did about Heaven, but, according to Rob, that was all hyperbole (exaggerating to get a point across) and Jesus really won't send anyone to hell for eternity. In fact, Rob says that people make their own hell by not trusting God, and most of this hell is what they experience while they are still here on earth.

What is Rob really doing in this book? He is making a god in his own image, one that loves him so much that he can't bear to disappoint him. But that's not love! Giving your children everything they want is the opposite of love. We cannot remake God the way we want Him. God is God and we are not. We cannot change the Bible to make it more palatable for people. We need to have faith that God will use His Word as it is to

> We cannot remake God the way we want Him.

accomplish what He wants. He did not ask us to figure out ways to change His gospel to make it politically correct. When we do that we are making a smaller god–a god who lives for us.

Rob sees humans as the center of the universe. While we are important in God's economy, He is using us to show His manifold wisdom to the angels, good and bad. God is the center of all things. The story is His story and not ours, and we can't change it.

Rob also falls into the trap that many others have of judging whether God is good or not. He says that a good God would not send anyone to Hell for eternity. He thinks that God is only love, like God is only holy. God has nothing in His personality that is the opposite of His holiness, but God has something in His personality that is the opposite of love. He says, "*Jacob have I loved, but Esau have I hated.* Romans 9:13. God is love but He also hates. He hates a false witness and the person who sows discord among brethren.

The psalmist says, *"Do not I hate them, O LORD that hate thee? And am not I grieved with those that rise up against thee? I hate them with perfect hatred: I count them my enemies."* Psalm 139:21, 22. Is the psalmist wrong, or is he doing exactly what God wants? There is absolutely nothing to indicate that he is doing anything but what God wants Him to do. Are we to love our enemies? Yes, and hate their sin–but we are to hate God's enemies. We should hate Satan and all he represents.

So God's holiness is absolute, but while God is love, His love is not absolute. If you don't want a God like that, you can start your own religion and make up your own god. The problem is that your god will just be a figment of your imagination.

Rob goes on to talk about Jesus' story of the rich man and Lazarus. He claims that Jesus is just trying to get the point across that we need to die to our realities and live to Christ's. He says on page 77:

"How do you communicate a story that complex and multilayered? You tell a nuanced, shocking story about a rich man and a poor man, and you throw in gruesome details about dogs licking his sores, and then you tell about a massive reversal in their deaths in which the rich man in hell has the ability to converse with Abraham, the father of the faith. And then you end it all with a twist about resurrection, a twist that is actually a hint about something that is going to happen in real history soon after this parable is told. Brilliant, just brilliant."

So Rob is again saying that this is hyperbole, just a gruesome parable to get a point across. The problem with that view is that Jesus never used a person's name in a parable. Jesus is telling a true story of what happened to two people who were probably known by the listeners. Why else give the name of the beggar? Let's take a look at the story:

Luke 16:19-31 *There was a certain rich man, who was clothed in purple and fine linen, and fared sumptuously every day: and there was a certain beggar named Lazarus, which was laid at his gate, full of sores, and desiring to be fed with the crumbs which fell from the rich man's table: moreover the dogs came and licked his sores.*

And it came to pass, that the beggar died, and was carried by the angels into Abraham's bosom: the rich man also died, and was buried; and in hell he lifted up his eyes, being in torment, and saw Abraham afar off, and Lazarus in his bosom.

Abraham's bosom, also called Paradise was where believers were taken when they died because the final sacrifice had not been made. Once Jesus died and went to Paradise Himself, He took them to Heaven. Those in Hell are still there in torment awaiting judgment.

And he cried and said, "Father Abraham, have mercy on me, and send Lazarus that he may dip the tip of his finger in water, and cool my tongue; for I am tormented in this flame."

Notice that there is a real flame and that the rich man is tormented, not just by his thoughts, as Rob says, but by the heat of a flame.

But Abraham said, "Son, remember that you in your lifetime received your good things, and likewise Lazarus evil things: but now he is comforted, and you are tormented. And beside all this, between us and you there is a great gulf fixed: so that they which would pass from here to you cannot; neither can they pass to us that would come from there."

Then he said, "I pray you therefore, father, that you would send him to my father's house: for I have five brothers; that he may testify unto them, lest they also come into this place of torment".

When a person dies, no matter where he goes, he wants his loved ones to go to heaven.

Abraham said unto him, "They have Moses and the prophets; let them hear them."

And he said, "No, father Abraham: but if one went unto them from the dead, they will repent."

This is a common misconception.

And he said unto him, "If they hear not Moses and the prophets, neither will they be persuaded, though one rose from the dead."

A very interesting statement; why is this true? If we come to God based on our free will, then the more info we get, the more likely we will be to believe. On the other hand, if we come because God has chosen, called, drawn, and made us alive, then this statement makes perfect sense.

There is nothing in this story that indicates it is anything but a retelling of an actual happening. Two people, Lazarus and Abraham, are specifically named in this story–again, that is something Jesus never did in a parable. Why is the rich man not named? I think it is because he went to Hell and only those who were believers are named because they had eternal life and were in Paradise. I don't think the listeners to this story had any trouble figuring out who the rich man was. They all knew where Lazarus had begged for years. Sorry Rob, this story is not just about getting the rich man to realize that Lazarus is his equal.

Rob uses the Hebrew and Greek words for "forever and ever" to show that they don't really mean forever, but ages upon ages. Then he says that we use ages about short-term things that only seem like ages. Literally he is correct; however, "ages upon ages" is an idiom which the people of that day understood as "forever". We always need to interpret scripture in the way it was meant for the original readers as the primary interpretation.

We use idioms all of the time in English which confuses those who are learning our language. "A dime a dozen" is a good example of an idiom. We all know that we don't literally mean that the things being described are less than a penny each, but that they are plentiful and worth less because they are so easily obtained.

That is the point of an idiom. The people who use it understand it, and their understanding determines the meaning and interpretation.

Then Rob quotes church fathers and leaders whom he claims believed as he does. Some well may have had universalist beliefs, but that does not change the truth. He quotes a letter from Martin Luther talking about a possible second chance and quotes Luther as writing, "Who could doubt God's ability to do that." So Rob takes a possibility from a private letter to say that Luther may have believed in second chances, but throws out the strong, essential teaching of Luther on which the reformation was based. Here is a quote from "*Bondage of the Will*" by Martin Luther under the heading, "*The Sovereignty of God.*"

"Sect. 9.—THIS, therefore, is also essentially necessary and wholesome for Christians to know: That God foreknows nothing by contingency, but that He foresees, purposes, and does all things according to His immutable, eternal, and infallible will. By this thunderbolt, 'Free will' is thrown prostrate, and utterly dashed to pieces. Those, therefore, who would assert 'Free will,' must either deny this thunderbolt, or pretend not to see it, or push it from them."

Rob's whole premise is that we, in our free will, can come to God and God is desperately trying to get us to come. Rob is so far to the left of Erasmus, the church leader whom Luther is correcting, that he isn't even in the same ballpark. Erasmus said that in the sinful human heart there is the smallest speck of goodness that can enable it to turn to God. He calls this free will, and Luther writes a whole book to prove that there is not even a speck of a possibility of goodness in us. Rob thinks that we generally are not all that bad, and God just needs to reform us so we can be with Him forever.

The truth is that we are so bad that we must die so that our new nature, God's righteousness, can take over. Jesus said. "You must be born again," not "You must be reformed." And we can't do that. God alone saves us. He does it by making us alive while we could do nothing because we were dead.

Rob does get some things right, but when he writes that we will spend eternity on this earth, he is only half right. There will be a thousand year reign of Jesus Christ, here on earth, which will end with millions teaming up with Satan to attempt to overthrow His Kingdom. This time Jesus won't waste time fighting, He will just burn them all up. Then the earth will be destroyed, and a new heaven and earth will be created. The New Jerusalem will come down from God out of Heaven, and God will dwell with us there forever.

The important thing is that as we, through faith, speak of the Christ of scripture. We need to speak the truth and never compromise to be politically correct or make the gospel easier to swallow. We need to put our faith in the One who can save anyone He chooses. Our arguments, reasoning, and logic will save no one, though He may use them as part of the process.

As we have seen, there are two sides of the horse from which to fall. Some add false beliefs to the Gospel, which make it harder to believe–like the young earth science guys. And there are those, like Rob, who want to make it so easy that you don't even have to make a decision in this life, just enjoy life and change your mind after you die.

I cannot think of a worse possible sin than this: to tell people there is a second chance when there is not. I suppose that the only thing that would match it, would be to tell people that you are "the way, the truth, and the life" if you are not. It would be far less heinous for a doctor to give a person a clean bill of health when he knows he has cancer and could be cured, because that is only temporal, not eternal. I believe Rob's name may become a curse word in hell for those who have believed this lie.

> I cannot think of a worse possible sin than to tell people there is a second chance when there is not.

We need to proclaim the truth of the gospel. It is the truth that sets people free. We need to have the faith it takes to speak this truth to those around us. We should make it a HABIT to pray every day for the following five things:

1. **H**ave opportunities to speak to those who do not yet know Christ.
2. **A**bility to recognize the opportunity before it's too late.
3. **B**oldness to take the opportunity.
4. **I**nterest in the person, not the mission
5. **T**rust in the Holy Spirit for what to say instead of leaning on our own understanding.

If we will regularly pray for these things and obey, we will be amazed at what God will do through us for those around us.

Chapter Seven

Faith that Enjoys

There is a small story in the life of Samson that is quite interesting. Samson has found a Philistine girl who "pleases him well". Incidentally, the Israelites were not to marry the heathen, so this was a sin, and yet the Bible says it was from God because He was seeking an occasion against the Philistines. Samson and his parents went to Timnath, where she lived, but on the way, while separated from his parents, a young lion attacked him. The Spirit of the Lord came upon Samson and he killed the lion as he would have killed a kid of the goats. When he rejoined his parents, he didn't tell them what had happened.

Some time later, as Samson and his parents came to his wedding, Samson turned aside to see the lion and found a honeybee's hive in the carcass of the lion. Now that doesn't happen! Bees will not nest in a dead animal that has any flesh on it, or even if it still smells like rotten meat. If there are no trees around, bees might nest in a bleached skeleton, but it would be quite unusual. It would have to be a very long time for the bones of the carcass to bleach and for the bees to make enough honey for Samson to share with his parents. I believe that this was clearly a miracle. Samson took some of the honey and gave it to his parents, but didn't tell them where he got it. Also notice that Samson violated the Nazarite vow by touching a dead animal.

At the wedding there were thirty male companions, and Samson gave them a challenge. If they could explain his riddle by the end of the seven day feast, he would give each of them a change of clothing, but if they could not, they each would owe him a change of clothing. They accepted, so he told them the riddle:

Out of the eater came forth meat,
Out of the strong came forth sweetness.

The guys couldn't figure it out so they, in true bully fashion, threatened Samson's wife that if she didn't find out the answer, they would burn her and her father's house. She cried for the rest of the week that if Samson loved her, he would tell her the answer to the riddle. On the last day Samson couldn't take it anymore and told her the answer. She promptly told the guys and they triumphantly related to Samson the answer. He got angry and killed thirty other Philistines and stripped them to give his companions changes of clothing. Samson was so disgusted with his new wife that he moved back home without her.

Why do I tell you this story, and what does it have to do with enjoyment? It's another allegory! The story happened exactly the way it's written in scripture, but the God who controls all things has a story within a story. The lion is the Lion of the tribe of Judah, Jesus Christ. Samson is a sinner taking responsibility for the death of

Jesus, and he finds miraculous sustenance and sweetness through the death and resurrection (life from death as seen in the bees in the carcass) of Jesus. The world (his parents) doesn't know from where the sweetness comes, but enjoys it, as so much goodness in the world comes from Christians and their values.

It is because of the gospel that there are so many schools and hospitals in this world. The majority of our most respected schools, like Harvard, Yale, and Oxford, were started for the sole purpose of training pastors how to study the Bible and preach. Many of our great hospitals were started by believers in Jesus Christ as well. I have seen a quote several times, though I cannot verify it, that more hospitals have been started by Christians than by all other religions combined. Many other values come from Christianity that benefit unbelievers. However, too many believers are like Samson and never tell anyone where they got the sweetness, but they never fully experience it until they do.

For the believer, this miraculous sustenance and sweetness can be appreciated whether things are going well or terrible. It is not dependent on

> If we see our earthly lives as all-important, our comfort as primary, and our pleasure as a reason to live; we will never taste this sweetness.

circumstances, but it is dependent on attitudes. If we see our earthly lives as all-important, our comfort as primary, and our pleasure as a reason to live, we will never taste this sweetness. But if we truly give up our lives to Him who gave His life for us, view comfort and pleasure as things that belong in the next life and are only fleeting here, learn that life here is about loving God and loving people–and serving God and serving people–we will find that sustenance and sweetness that comes only from the death and resurrection of the Lion of the tribe of Judah.

If we can view every trial and every problem as coming from our loving Father for His good purposes and for His glory; then nothing can stop the sweetness of His presence and the intimacy of His friendship.

Epilogue

I realize that there is so much more to say, but if I keep going, this book will be too long and it won't be read by as many people. My desire is for all of us to see the true God as He is, and not as we would like to make Him, so that we can worship with our brain as well as our heart.

True Christianity is the only religion where you don't have to check your brain at the door, yet many teachers and leaders teach things that don't make sense, don't follow scripture, and are scientifically incorrect. We need to start using our God-given brains to make sure that our interpretation of scripture is logical and fits with scripture and true science.

Don't misunderstand, I am not saying we can understand God any more than He wants us to understand Him, or that miracles don't happen. It is quite logical that finite human beings cannot understand an infinite God any more than He wishes to reveal Himself to them, and it is also quite logical that the God who created all things can do anything He wants to do, whenever He wants. I just want us to think things through before we teach them.

As I finish this book, typed with only my left hand–my right wrist is still in a cast which will come off in three to five weeks–the ribs are much better and I have another nice scar on the back of my head. The doctor says that I have about a poor chance of the bones surviving, but my God is unlimited and He will do as He sees fit, and I will thank Him. I am praying that I will continue to serve Him more faithfully no matter where He takes me.

At Celebrate Recovery last night the topic was "Gratitude." When it was my turn to share, I said that I was very grateful to be brought up in a wonderful, loving, Christian home, and also grateful to have been trapped in pornography for years, because now I know my own depravity and that there is no sinner on the planet worse than I am. This makes it easy for me to forgive others and to forgive myself. Pride keeps us from forgiving ourselves and others. I can be truly thankful for the worst things because my God is in control and has a good purpose in what He brings into my life. I am so grateful to Him for all He is doing in and through me.

> Pride keeps us from forgiving ourselves and others.

God bless you greatly as you ponder Who really is the God of the Bible, and learn to trust Him more and draw ever closer to Him.

www.ingramcontent.com/pod-product-compliance
Lightning Source LLC
Chambersburg PA
CBHW061739020426
42331CB00006B/1295